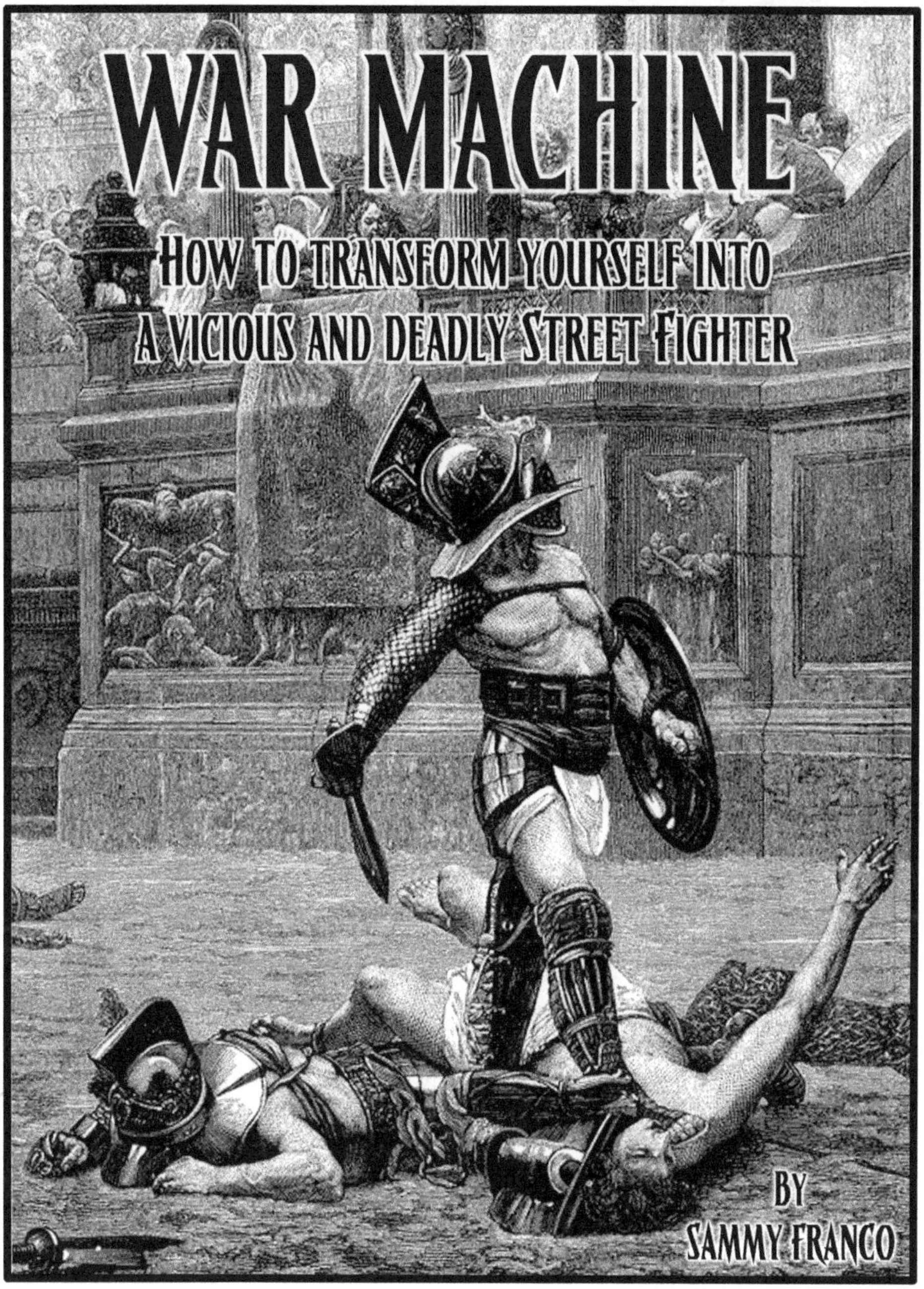

Also by Sammy Franco:

Heavy Bag Training: Boxing - Mixed Martial Arts - Self Defense
Out of the Cage
Gun Safety: For Home Defense and Concealed Carry
Warrior Wisdom: Inspiring Ideas from the World's Greatest Warriors
Savage Street Fighting: Tactical Savagery as a Last Resort
Ground War: How to Destroy a Grappler in a Street Fight
Feral Fighting: Level 2 WidowMaker
The Combat Conditioning Workout Journal
War Blade: A Complete Guide to Tactical Knife Fighting
The WidowMaker Program: Maximum Punishment for Extreme Situations
War Craft: Street Fighting Tactics of the War Machine
The Bigger They Are, The Harder They Fall:
First Strike: Mastering the Pre-Emptive Strike for Street Combat
1001 Street Fighting Secrets: The Principles of Contemporary Fighting Arts
When Seconds Count: Everyone's Guide to Self-Defense
Killer Instinct: Unarmed Combat for Street Survival
Street Lethal: Unarmed Urban Combat

War Machine: How to Transform Yourself into a Vicious and Deadly Street Fighter by Sammy Franco

Copyright © 2001-2014 by Sammy Franco

ISBN: 978-098187210-0

Published by Contemporary Fighting Arts, LLC
P.O. Box 84028
Gaithersburg, Maryland 20883
Phone: (301) 279-2244

All rights reserved. Except for use in a review, no portion
of this book may be reproduced in any form without the
express written permission of the publisher.

Direct inquiries and/or orders to the above address.

Neither the author nor the publisher assumes any responsibility for the use or misuse of information contained in this book.

Book concept and photo selection by Sammy Franco.

For author interviews, or other publicity information, please send inquiries in care of the publisher or visit our web site at www.sammyfranco.com

Table of Contents

Preface

Introduction: Contemporary Fighting Arts

PART I: War Machine Psychology

PART II: War Machine Physiology

PART III: War Machine Combatives

PART IV: War Machine Philosophy

Appendix A: Battle Casualties

Appendix B: Code of Conduct

Appendix C: War Machine Glossary

About The Author

Dedication

This book is dedicated to the War Machine.

Warning!

The information and techniques presented herein can be dangerous and could result in serious injury and death. The author, publisher, and distributors of this book disclaim any liability from the damage or injuries of any type that a reader or user of information contained within this book may occur from the use of said information. This book is for academic study only.

Before you begin any diet or exercise program, including those suggested in this book, it is important to check with your physician to see if you have any condition that might be aggravated by a reducing diet or strenuous exercise.

Preface!

Congratulations! The fact that you have purchased this book and are reading it sets you apart from millions of other people. By choosing the War Machine program, you have made a calculated choice to change and ultimately improve yourself.

The book that you are holding in your hands will change you for the rest of your life. War Machine is a unique training program specifically designed to transform you into a vicious and powerful fighter. When followed accordingly, this program will forge your mind, body and spirit into iron.

Once armed with the mental and physical tools of the War Machine, you will become a strong and confident person that can handle just about anything that life may throw your way. In essence, War Machine is a way of life: Powerful, intense, and hard.

War Machine is divided into four unique chapters. Each one covering a critical aspect of the combat training. Part I: War Machine Psychology provides the mental and psychological tools to confidently handle the rigors of both armed and unarmed combat. Topics include, developing the "hard core" attitude, improving self-confidence, decisiveness, follow through, courage, combative desensitization, viciousness, self discipline, philosophical resolution, emotional masking, overcoming combat related stress reactions, visualization techniques, and much more!

Part II: War Machine Physiology covers the physical elements of the warrior, including the importance of appearance, combat body compositions, warm-ups, stretching, strength training exercises, split workout routines, combative utility of muscle groups, cardio conditioning, working with training partners, coping with pain, rest and burnout, and diet and nutrition.

Part III: War Machine Combatives will arm you with the concepts and principles necessary to master the warrior's arsenal. Here, you will learn about range proficiency, combat stances, strategic positioning, footwork, target orientation, target recognition, target selection, target impaction, target exploitation, target zones, medical implications of combat techniques, speed, impact power, ambidexterity, improving offensive reaction time, balance, non-telegraphic movement, first strike, auto pilot fighting, and the killer instinct.

Part IV: War Machine Philosophy bridges the gap between the technical and philosophical aspects of combat with a chapter devoted to the philosophy of warfare. Subjects include courage, pacifism, good vs. evil, the ego, laws of reality, loyalty, leadership, honor, frustration, and combat strategies.

At the end of this book I have included a couple appendices that you should take a look at. Finally, since most of the terminology used in this text is defined within the context of Contemporary Fighting Arts (CFA), I have provided an elaborate glossary. Welcome to the War Machine program!

Sammy Franco
Gaithersburg, Maryland
February 18, 2014

Introduction

What is Contemporary Fighting Arts?

Contemporary Fighting Arts® (CFA), is a state-of-the-art combat system founded in 1989. This sophisticated and practical system of self-defense is designed specifically to provide efficient and effective methods to avoid, defuse, confront, and neutralize both armed and unarmed assailants in a variety of deadly situations and circumstances.

Unlike mixed martial arts, karate, or kung-fu, CFA is an offensive-based martial art system that is specifically designed for the violence that plagues our city streets. CFA dispenses with the extraneous and the impractical and focuses on real-life street fighting.

Every tool, technique and tactic found within the CFA system must meet three essential criteria for fighting: efficiency, effectiveness, and safety. Efficiency means that the techniques permit you to reach your combative objective quickly and economically. Effectiveness means that the elements of the system will produce the desired effect. Finally, safety means that the combative elements provide the least amount of danger and risk for you - the fighter.

CFA is not about tournaments or competition. It does not require you to waste time and energy practicing forms (katas) or other impractical rituals. There are no theatrical kicks or exotic techniques. And finally, CFA does not adhere blindly to tradition for tradition's sake. Simply put, it is a scientific yet pragmatic approach to staying alive on the streets.

CFA has been taught to people of all walks of life. Some include the U.S. Border Patrol, police officers, deputy sheriffs, security guards, military personnel, private investigators, surgeons, lawyers, college professors, airline pilots as well as black belts, boxers, and kick boxers. CFA's broad appeal results from its ability to teach people how to really fight.

IT'S ALL IN THE NAME!

Before discussing the three components that make up Contemporary Fighting Arts, it is important to understand how CFA acquired its unique name. To begin, the first word, "Contemporary," was selected because it refers to the system's modern, up-to-date orientation. Unlike traditional martial arts, CFA is specifically designed to meet the challenges of our modern world.

The second term, "Fighting," was chosen because it accurately describes the system's combat orientation. After all, why not just call it Contemporary Martial Arts? There are two reasons for this. First, the word "martial" conjures up images of traditional and impractical martial art forms that are antithetical to the system. Second, why dilute a perfectly functional name when the word "fighting" defines the system so succinctly? Contemporary Fighting Arts is about teaching people how to really fight.

Police officers need practical and effective defensive tactics for dealing with vicious street criminals. This is why many law enforcement officers come to Contemporary Fighting Arts for training.

Let's look at the last word, "Arts." In the subjective sense, "art" refers to the combat skills that are acquired through arduous study, practice, and observation. The bottom line is that effective street fighting skills will require consistent practice and attention. Take, for example, something as seemingly basic as an elbow strike, which will actually require hundreds of hours of practice to perfect.

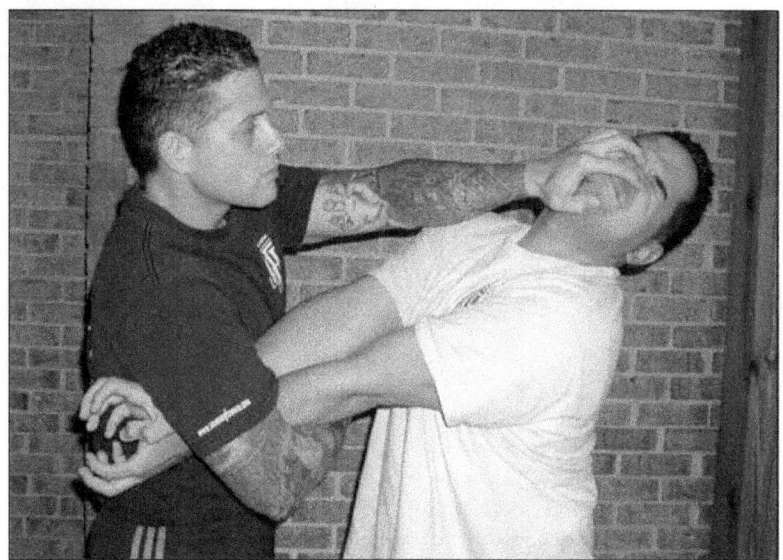

Contemporary Fighting Arts (CFA) is more than a self defense system, its a one-of-a-kind martial arts style geared for real world self defense.

The pluralization of the word "Art" reflects CFA's protean instruction. The various components of CFA's training (i.e., firearms training, stick fighting, ground fighting, natural body weapon mastery, and so on) have all truly earned their status as individual art forms and, as such, require years of consistent study and practice to perfect.

To acquire a greater understanding of CFA, here is an overview of the system's three vital components: the physical, the mental, and the spiritual.

Contemporary Fighting Arts (CFA) has a several unique military combat training programs. Our mission is to provide today's modern soldier with the knowledge, skills and attitude necessary to survive a wide variety of real world combat scenarios. Our military self defense program is designed to provide the modern soldier with the safest and most effective skills and tactics to control and decentralize armed and unarmed enemies.

THE PHYSICAL COMPONENT

The physical component of CFA focuses on the physical development of a fighter, including physical fitness, weapon and technique mastery, and self-defense attributes.

Physical Fitness

If you are going to prevail in a street fight, you must be physically fit. It's that simple. In fact, you will never master the tools and skills of combat unless you're in excellent physical shape. On the average, you will have to spend more than an hour a day to achieve maximum fitness.

In CFA physical fitness comprises the following three broad components: cardiorespiratory conditioning, muscular/skeletal conditioning, and proper body composition.

The cardiorespiratory system includes the heart, lungs, and circulatory system, which undergo tremendous stress during the course of a street fight. So you're going to have to run, jog, bike, swim, or skip rope to develop sound cardiorespiratory conditioning. Each aerobic workout should last a minimum of 30 minutes and be performed at least four times per week.

The second component of physical fitness is muscular/skeletal conditioning. In the streets, the strong survive and the rest go to the morgue. To strengthen your bones and muscles to withstand the rigors of a real fight, your program must include progressive resistance (weight training) and calisthenics. You will also need a stretching program designed to loosen up every muscle group. You can't kick, punch, ground fight, or otherwise execute the necessary body mechanics if you're "tight" or inflexible. Stretching on a regular basis will also increase the muscles' range of motion, improve circulation, reduce the possibility of injury, and relieve daily stress.

The final component of physical fitness is proper body composition: simply, the ratio of fat to lean body tissue. Your diet and training regimen will affect your level or percentage of body fat significantly. A sensible and consistent exercise program accompanied by a healthy and balanced diet will facilitate proper body composition. Don't neglect this important aspect of physical fitness.

WEAPON AND TECHNIQUE MASTERY

You won't stand a chance against a vicious assailant if you don't master the weapons and tools of fighting. In CFA, we teach our students both armed and unarmed methods of combat. Unarmed fighting requires that you master a complete arsenal of natural body weapons and techniques. In conjunction, you must also learn the various stances, hand positioning, footwork, body mechanics, defensive structure, locks, chokes, and various holds. Keep in mind that something as simple as a basic punch will actually require hundreds of hours to perfect.

Range proficiency is another important aspect of weapon and technique mastery. Briefly, range proficiency is the ability to fight effectively in all three ranges of unarmed fighting. Although punching range tools are emphasized in CFA, kicking and grappling ranges cannot be neglected. Our kicking range tools consist of deceptive and powerful low-line kicks. Grappling range tools include head-butts, elbows, knees, foot stomps, biting, tearing, gouging, and crushing tactics.

Although CFA focuses on striking, we also teach our students a myriad of chokes, locks, and holds that can be used in a ground fight. While such grappling range submission techniques are not the most preferred methods of dealing with a ground fighting situation, they must be studied for the following six reasons: (1) level of force - many ground fighting situations do not justify the use of deadly force. In such instances, you must apply various non-lethal submission holds, (2) nature of the beast - in order to escape any choke, lock or hold, you must first know how to apply them yourself, (3) occupational requirement- some professional occupations (police, security, etc.) require that you possess a working knowledge of various submission techniques, (4) subduing a friend or relative - in many cases it is best to restrain and control a friend or relative with a submission hold instead of striking him with a natural body weapon, (5) anatomical orientation - practicing various chokes, locks and holds will help you develop a strong orientation of the human anatomy, and (6) refutation requirement - finally, if you are going to criticize the combative limitations of any submission hold, you better be sure that you can perform it yourself.

Defensive tools and skills are also taught. Our defensive structure is efficient, uncomplicated, and impenetrable. It provides the fighter maximum protection while allowing complete freedom of choice for acquiring offensive control. Our defensive structure is based on distance, parrying, blocking, evading, mobility, and stance structure. Simplicity is always the key.

Students are also instructed in specific methods of armed fighting. For example, CFA provides instruction about firearms for personal and household protection. We provide specific guidelines for handgun purchasing, operation, nomenclature, proper caliber, shooting fundamentals, cleaning, and safe storage. Our firearm program also focuses on owner responsibility and the legal ramifications regarding the use of deadly force. CFA's weapons program also consists of natural body weapons, knives and edged weapons, single and double stick, makeshift weaponry, the side-handle baton, and oleoresin capsicum (OC) spray.

COMBAT ATTRIBUTES

Your offensive and defensive tools are useless unless they are used strategically. For any tool or technique to be effective in a real fight, it must be accompanied by specific attributes. Attributes are qualities that enhance a particular tool, technique, or maneuver. Some examples include speed, power, timing, coordination, accuracy, non-telegraphic movement, balance, and target orientation.

CFA also has a wide variety of training drills and methodologies designed to develop and sharpen these combat attributes. For example, our students learn to ground fight while blindfolded, spar with one arm tied down, and fight while handcuffed.

Reality is the key. For example, in class students participate in full-contact exercises against fully padded assailants, and real weapon disarms are rehearsed and analyzed in a variety of dangerous scenarios. Students also train with a large variety of equipment, including heavy bags, double-end bags, uppercut bags, pummel bags, focus mitts, striking shields, mirrors, rattan sticks, foam and plastic bats, kicking pads, training knives, trigger-sensitive (mock) guns, boxing and digit gloves, full-body armor, and hundreds of different environmental props.

There are more than 200 unique training methodologies used in CFA. Each one is scientifically designed to prepare students for the hard-core realities of combat. There are also three specific training methodologies used to develop and sharpen the fundamental attributes and skills of armed and unarmed fighting, including proficiency training, conditioning training, and street training.

Proficiency training can be used for both armed and unarmed skills. When conducted properly, proficiency training develops speed, power, accuracy, non-telegraphic movement, balance, and general psychomotor skill. The training objective is to sharpen one specific body weapon, maneuver, or technique at a time by executing it over and over for a prescribed number of repetitions. Each time the technique or maneuver is executed with "clean" form at various speeds. Movements are also performed with the eyes closed to develop a kinesthetic "feel" for the action. Proficiency training can be accomplished through the use of various types of equipment, including the heavy bag, double-end bag, focus mitts, training knives, real and mock pistols, striking shields, shin and knee guards, foam and plastic bats, mannequin heads, and so on.

Conditioning training develops endurance, fluidity, rhythm, distancing, timing, speed, footwork, and balance. In most cases, this type of training requires the student to deliver a variety of fighting combinations for three- or four-minute rounds separated by 30-second breaks. Like proficiency training, this type of training can also be performed at various speeds. A good workout consists of at least five rounds. Conditioning training can be performed on the bags with full-contact sparring gear, rubber training knives, focus mitts, kicking shields, and shin guards, or against imaginary assailants in shadow fighting.

Conditioning training is not necessarily limited to just three- or four-minute rounds. For example, CFA's ground fighting training can last as long as 30 minutes. The bottom line is that it all depends on what you are training for.

Street training is the final preparation for the real thing. Since many violent altercations are explosive, lasting an average of 20 seconds, you must prepare for this possible scenario. This means delivering explosive and powerful compound attacks with vicious intent for approximately 20 seconds, resting one minute, and then repeating the process.

Street training prepares you for the stress and immediate fatigue of a real fight. It also develops speed, power, explosiveness, target selection and recognition, timing, footwork, pacing, and breath control. You should practice this methodology in different lighting, on different terrains, and in different environmental settings. You can use different types of training equipment as well.

For example, you can prepare yourself for multiple assailants by having your training partners attack you with focus mitts from a variety of angles, ranges, and target postures. For 20 seconds, go after them with vicious low-line kicks, powerful punches, and devastating strikes.

When all is said and done, the physical component creates a fighter who is physically fit and armed with a lethal arsenal of tools, techniques, and weapons that can be deployed with destructive results.

THE MENTAL COMPONENT

The mental component of CFA focuses on the cerebral aspects of a fighter, developing killer instinct, strategic/tactical awareness, analysis and integration skills, philosophy, and cognitive skills.

The Killer Instinct

Deep within each of us is a cold and deadly primal power known as the "killer instinct." The killer instinct is a vicious combat mentality that surges to your consciousness and turns you into a fierce fighter who is free of fear, anger, and apprehension. If you want to survive the horrifying dynamics of real criminal violence, you must cultivate and utilize this instinctive killer mentality.

There are 14 unique characteristics of CFA's killer instinct. They are as follows: (1) clear and lucid thinking, (2) heightened situational awareness, (3) adrenaline surge, (4) mobilized body, (5) psychomotor control, (6) absence of distraction, (7) tunnel vision, (8) fearless mind-set, (9) tactical implementation, (10) the lack of emotion, (11) breath control, (12) pseudospeciation, (13) viciousness, and (14) pain tolerance.

In CFA we strive to tap the killer instinct in everyone. Visualization and crisis rehearsal are just two techniques used to develop, refine, and channel this extraordinary source of strength and energy so that it can be used to its full potential.

Strategic/Tactical Awareness

Strategy is the bedrock of preparedness. In CFA, there are three unique categories of strategic awareness that will diminish the likelihood of criminal victimization. They are criminal awareness, situational awareness, and self-awareness. When developed, these essential skills prepare you to assess a wide variety of threats instantaneously and accurately. Once you've made a proper threat assessment, you will be able to choose one of the following five self-defense options: comply, escape, de-escalate, assert, or fight back.

CFA also teaches students to assess a variety of other important factors, including the assailant's demeanor, intent, range, positioning and weapon capability, as well as such environmental issues as escape routes, barriers, terrain, and makeshift weaponry. In addition to assessment skills, CFA also teaches students how to enhance perception and observation skills.

Analysis and Integration Skills

The analytical process is intricately linked to understanding how to defend yourself in any threatening situation. If you want to be the best, every aspect of fighting and personal protection must be dissected. Every strategy, tactic, movement, and concept must be broken down to its atomic parts. The three planes (physical, mental, spiritual) of self-defense must be unified scientifically through arduous practice and constant exploration.

CFA's most advanced practitioners have sound insight and understanding of a wide range of sciences and disciplines. They include human anatomy, kinesiology, criminal justice, sociology, kinesics, proxemics, combat physics, emergency medicine, crisis management, histrionics, police and military science, the psychology of aggression, and the role of archetypes.

Analytical exercises are also a regular part of CFA training. For example, we conduct problem-solving sessions involving particular assailants attacking in defined environments. We move hypothetical attackers through various ranges to provide insight into tactical solutions. We scrutinize different methods of attack for their general utility in combat. We also discuss the legal ramifications of self-defense on a frequent basis.

In addition to problem-solving sessions, students are slowly exposed to concepts of integration and modification. Oral and written examinations are given to measure intellectual accomplishment.

Philosophy

Philosophical resolution is essential to a fighter's mental confidence and clarity. Anyone learning the art of war must find the ultimate answers to questions concerning the use of violence in defense of himself or others. To advance to the highest levels of combat awareness, you must find clear and lucid answers to such provocative questions as could you take the life of another, what are your fears, who are you, why are you interested in studying Contemporary Fighting Arts, why are you reading this book, and what is good and what is evil? If you haven't begun the quest to formulate these important questions and answers, then take a break. It's time to figure out just why you want to know the laws and rules of destruction.

Cognitive Skills

Cognitive exercises are also important for improving one's fighting skills. CFA uses visualization and crisis rehearsal scenarios to improve general body mechanics, tools and techniques, and maneuvers, as well as tactic selection. Mental clarity, concentration, and emotional control are also developed to enhance one's ability to call upon the controlled killer instinct.

THE SPIRITUAL COMPONENT

There are many tough fighters out there. In fact, they reside in every town in every country. However, most are nothing more than vicious animals that lack self-mastery. And self-mastery is what separates the true warrior from the eternal novice.

I am not referring to religious precepts or beliefs when I speak of CFA's spiritual component. Unlike most martial arts, CFA does not merge religion into its spiritual aspect. Religion is a very personal and private matter and should never, ever be incorporated into any fighting system.

CFA's spiritual component is not something that is taught or studied. Rather, it is that which transcends the physical and mental aspects of being and reality. There is a deeper part of each of us that is a tremendous source of truth and accomplishment.

While there are many dedicated individuals who are more than qualified to teach unique philosophical and spiritual components of ancient martial arts, you must realize that such forms of combat can get you killed in a real life self-defense encounter.

In CFA, the spiritual component is something that is slowly and progressively acquired. During the challenging quest of combat training, one begins to tap the higher qualities of human nature, those elements of our being that inherently enable us to know right from wrong and good from evil. As we slowly develop this aspect of our total self, we begin to strengthen qualities profoundly important to the "truth." Such qualities are essential to your growth through the mastery of inner peace, the clarity of your "vision," and your recognition of universal truths.

One of the goals of my system is to promote virtue and moral responsibility in people who have extreme capacities for physical and mental destructiveness. The spiritual component of fighting is truly the most difficult aspect of personal growth. Yet unlike the physical component, where the practitioner's abilities will be limited to some degree by genetics and other natural factors, the spiritual component of combat offers unlimited potential for growth and development. In the final analysis, CFA's spiritual component poses the greatest challenges for the student. It is an open-ended plane of unlimited advancement.

PART I
War Machine Psychology

"Civility is a Sweet poison that must be lanced and exorcised if you are ever to become the War Machine."

- Sammy Franco

Mental Toughness

There is a unique psychological dimension to the War Machine. He possesses personality traits that exceed far beyond the average person. During trying times, he can withstand great psychological strain without breaking down. He is always resolute and in full control of any situation. Simply put, the War Machine is mentally tough. Mental toughness is broken down into ten constituents. They are:

- **Hard Core Attitude**
- **Self Confidence**
- **Decisiveness**
- **Follow Through**
- **Courage**
- **Combative Desensitization**
- **Viciousness**
- **Self Discipline**
- **Philosophically Resolute**
- **Responsibility**

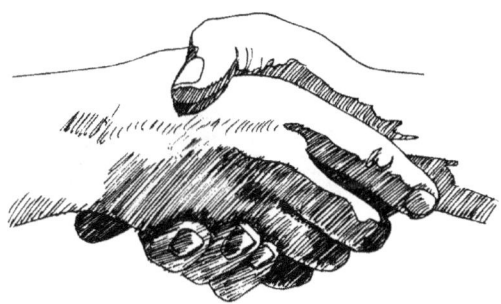

Everything about the War Machine is strong and forceful. Something as trivial as his handshake indicates a man of strength and confidence.

You may find that you already possess maybe one or two of these components, but it's a very rare case when all of these traits are naturally instilled in a person. While the average man isn't born with the complete mental toughness package, with proper training and determination, it can be learned and developed.

Don't confuse mental toughness with its cousin the killer instinct. While both have similar qualities, mental toughness is the stable internal climate that nourishes and ultimately spawns the killer instinct. Having said that, let's begin by looking at the attitude of the War Machine.

Hard Core Attitude

The attitude of a War Machine is simple. He doesn't take shit from anyone! He does not capitulate or prostrate to another. "Kissing ass" is never a consideration to this warrior. He takes pride in who he is and will assert himself whenever necessary. Some people erroneously assume that "having a chip on your shoulder" can provoke trouble, but in many situations it can significantly reduce the likelihood of a confrontation with a potential adversary.

The immutable fact is humans, by nature, take full advantage of weak and timid personalities. It's no surprise that meek people get manipulated and hurt by shrewd and psychologically dominant street criminals. These nefarious predators know what to look for and how to exploit it. They just love an easy mark.

However, when a criminal predator comes in contact with a War Machine, something very different takes place. The War Machine's carriage and movements reveal a person of purpose and conviction. Conversing with a War Machine, even if it's just for a few seconds, will immediately illustrate a person of strength and unshakable vigilance. The War Machine has a certain look in his eye that immediately deters even the most seasoned predator. And in no time at all, the would-be victimizer quickly moves on to find someone else.

The War Machine's carriage and movements reveal a person of purpose and conviction

The Necessity of Masking

The face we present to the world is rarely our real face.

One essential component of the War Machine's attitude is Masking. In essence, Masking is the process of concealing your true feelings from a potential adversary by manipulating and managing your body language (both facial and body expressions). Obviously, displaying signs of fear, anger, trepidation or weariness to a potential enemy can be disastrous for the War Machine.

Masking is a learned discipline that requires your constant attention. When faced with a potential enemy, you cannot afford to "let your guard down" or have a momentary lapse in your body language. You must be aware of yourself at all times.

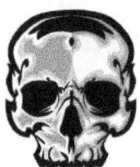

BEWARE! Masking too frequently often becomes a self-perpetuating process that is difficult to stop. Eventually the mask won't come off and this can be particularly troublesome in personal or intimate relationships. So remember to mask only when you absolutely have to!

While masking cannot cover or hide some involuntary physical reactions (i.e., excessive perspiring, heavy breathing, trembling hands and legs, etc.) you can cover them up by quickly moving about, diverting the assailant's attention elsewhere, etc.

Self Confidence

A War Machine believes in himself. He displays a strong sense of confidence in himself and his capacity to fight. His high degree of self-esteem prohibits him from entertaining thoughts of self-doubt or apprehension. In combat, the War Machine is optimistic about his ability to neutralize his adversary, despite the odds or circumstances.

Self-confidence is a significant component of mental toughness. It's no wonder that War Machines make great leaders.

Confidence is critical in combat because it permits you to fight in the face of extreme adversity. Generally speaking, a confident warrior is usually a fearless warrior. Finally, the greater your sense of self-confidence, the greater challenges you will be willing to undertake.

"A soldier who has proper confidence in his own skill and strength entertains no thought of mutiny." - Publius Flavius Vegetius Renatus

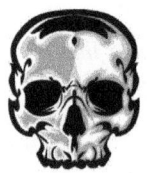 *Negative self-talk is one of the greatest saboteurs of self-confidence. Listening to these negative internal messages during battle will hinder your ability to fight. Make every effort to prevent these messages from entering your mind.*

Decisiveness

In combat, the War Machine not only knows what to do but when to do it. He is one who clearly demonstrates a strong sense of decisiveness both on and off the battlefield. While every decision involves some type of risk, the War Machine is resolute and able to make difficult decisions regardless of how grim the consequences might be.

Decisiveness is an indispensable trait that often promotes combative success. Indecisiveness, on the other hand, is usually a precursor to failure and possibly death. Decisiveness requires that you completely understand the entire issue at hand before making a decision. Rushing to conclusions when there is enough time to assess a particular situation is something that should be avoided. Above all, the decision making process should always be predicated on logic rather than emotion.

"I have with me two gods, Persuasion and Compulsion." -Themistocles

Follow-Through

Deep in the recesses of his mind, the War Machine has a burning desire to succeed and achieve his desired outcome. He is relentless in the pursuit of his personal goals and objectives. The War Machine does not need to be pushed or motivated from external sources. His passion and drive come from within. Setbacks are viewed as micro challenges. He simply does not dwell on them!

During training, even after the enthusiasm is gone, the War Machine has the follow-through to push forward and achieve his goal. Whatever he starts, he finishes! He doesn't know the meaning of the word quit.

In battle, follow-through can make the differences between winning and losing or living and dying. It's a trait that allows you to continue fighting, regardless of the harsh adversities that you're faced with.

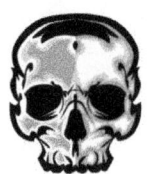

Death is inevitable when unqualified people are permitted to exercise judgment and make decisions on the battlefield.

Courage

Courage is another recognizable trait of the War Machine. Courageousness enables him to face danger with confidence, resolution, and bravery. In battle, the War Machine has the nerve to push through the fear that paralyzes most men. He realizes that succumbing to fear is worse than death itself.

In unarmed combat, when the War Machine is attacked and bombarded with punches and strikes, he never closes his eyes or reflexively drops his head. He knows that such a reaction would seal his fate. Instead, this warrior keeps his head erect and eyes wide open amid flying blows. If he gets hit, he doesn't panic. He just keeps moving, maintains proper breathing, applies the appropriate defensive response and counters swiftly when the window of opportunity presents itself.

"It is courage, courage, courage, that raises the blood of life to crimson splendor. Live bravely and present a brave front to adversity."-Horace

What is Fear?

Fear is a strong, unpleasant emotional reaction to a real or "perceived" threat. If uncontrolled, fear quickly leads to panic, and then it's too late to defend yourself in a fight. Here are a few tips to control the debilitating effects of fear:

(1) Become proficient with both armed and unarmed combat skills.
(2) Understand and accept the physiological responses of the fight-or-flight.
(3) Learn how to tap into and control your killer instinct.
(4) Stay in good physical shape.
(5) Always maintain a positive and analytical attitude in combat.
(6) During combat, be "tactical", not emotional!

The fearless King Leonidas of Sparta, Greece.

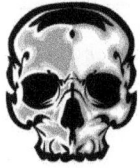 *Believe it or not, but your eyes are a sure give away when you're frightened. Avoid widening your eyes when faced with a threatening adversary. Instead, maintain a neutral and attentive facial expression that prevents the enemy from reading your intentions or feelings.*

Combative Desensitization

Warriors of the past were immune to violence and bloodshed. Unlike today's modern man who is civilized and acculturated.

There is very little question that combat is brutal and to the untrained fighter it can be downright horrifying. Actually, there are four stress-related phenomena or "reactions" that an untrained warrior will experience when faced with the sudden and intense trauma of combat. They include the following:

Surprise Reaction: The fighter is startled and instinctively "jumps" from the noise or action of combat. Essentially, the man is caught by surprise and reacts with involuntary "reflex" movements that delay his reaction time.

Distraction Reaction: The fighter's mind is inundated with internal distractions. He quickly becomes overwhelmed with self-doubt and he is apprehensive to take immediate action in the combat situation.

Break Down Reaction: Since the stress is too overwhelming for the fighter, his body literally breaks-down. He might experience dry mouth, inability to speak, sweaty hands, tight muscles, chest pain, feeling faint, nausea, vomiting, and uncontrolled urination or defecation.

Distortion Reaction: In terms of sights and sounds, the fighter perceives the combat situation unrealistically. He has a tendency to block out important visual and auditory elements of the fight. Moreover, his sense of time is distorted and he often has trouble recollecting the series of events that took place.

There's no doubt that such phenomena can be fatal for you in a combat situation. However, most people don't realize that such stress-related reactions will also create serious problems in the courtroom. For example, if you end up justifiably killing your adversary in a fight but cannot recall the situation in detail, or your story doesn't jive with witnesses or with the forensic evidence, you are going to raise some serious questions.

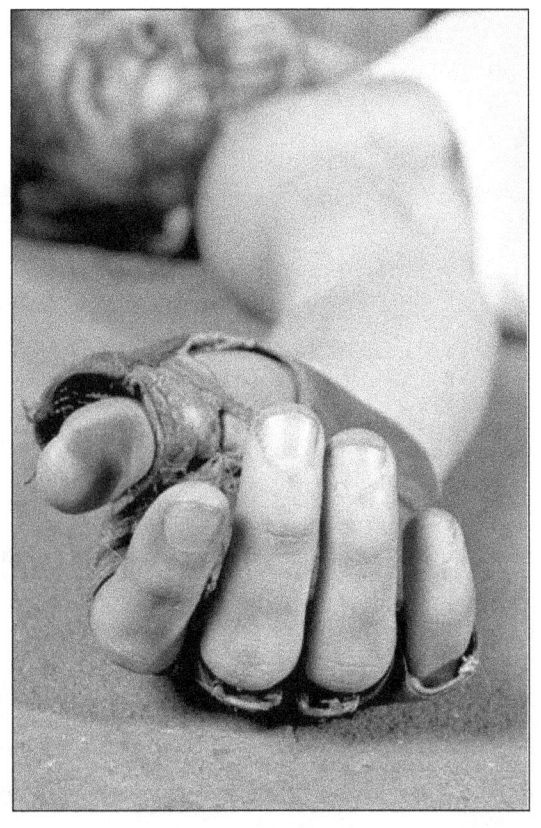

Despite what you may have seen in movies, A real street fight is bloody, ugly and brutal

The Stomach For Battle

The vast majority of street fights occur at close range. This means that you will most likely hear your enemy's bones break or get his blood splattered on your face and hands. Such horrid happenings can be extremely shocking and debilitating to those who are not combatively desensitized.

Fortunately, the War Machine has the stomach for battle and is habituated to its gruesome residuals. He anticipates the horror of combat and can work through it - he is combatively desensitized.

While there is no real substitute for actual fighting experience, combative desensitization can be developed. Through gradual exposure to increasing stressful combative stimuli, one can systematically lessen the stress producing reactions. It's just a question of proper self-defense training.

Keep in mind that the first step in becoming combatively desensitized is to first make yourself intellectually familiar with the characteristics of both armed and unarmed combat. What follows are the seven characteristics of combat:

(1) Combat is ugly, brutal and bloody.
(2) Combat is fast and explosive.
(3) Combat is unpredictable and spontaneous.
(4) Combat is extremely dangerous.
(5) Unarmed combat usually turns into a ground fight.
(6) Combat has no rules.
(7) Combat is almost always unfair.

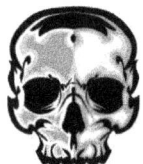

BEWARE: Your first combat experience is usually the one you never forget. If you have already experienced these negative combat phenomena and they have left you with unresolved fears, you must resolve them now or they will most likely be intensified the next time a combat situation occurs.

You Need To Visualize It!

Creative visualization is another effective method of helping you achieve combative desensitization. Visualization is the formation of mental images or pictures to improve your self-defense skills and abilities.

By frequently imagining yourself in various horrific combat scenarios, you are mentally familiarizing yourself with the look and feel of combat. As a result, the stress and "shock" of fighting (armed and unarmed) is significantly reduced. In essence, you are conditioning and programming your psychomotor system to respond effectively without freezing up or going into shock.

Research has proven that visual imagery causes brain activity identical to that produced by actual combat experience. Even if the image is unrealistic or surreal, your body will produce a response that stimulates every cell in your body. This is particularly important for people who want to become combatively desensitized but have never experienced actual combat.

Nevertheless, for visualization to work, you must make certain that your mental images are very clear, strong and consistent. You actually have to try to see, feel, taste, smell, and hear the visualized scenario. Effective visualization requires peace and quiet, so you'll need to find a place, free from distractions for at least 20 minutes.

Every visualization session must be undertaken in a relaxed state. To attain a state of relaxation you need to sit in a comfortable chair or lie on the couch or bed. If sitting, make certain your back is straight, arms uncrossed, and your feet are both on the floor. If lying down, place your arms at your sides.

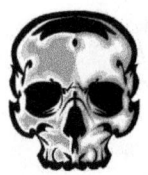
WARNING! Always remember that mental visualization is never a substitute for physical training. You must be able to physically perform the tools and techniques of combat before you can imagine using them.

Next, close your eyes and breath slowly and deeply for approximately two minutes. Then, tense every muscle in your body all at once. Clench your fists and feet. Tighten your jaw and facial muscles. Don't forget your shoulders, chest, back and legs. Hold this tension for approximately 10 seconds and then let go. Allow the tension to flow out of your body all at once. You are now ready to begin visualizing.

The Mental Movie

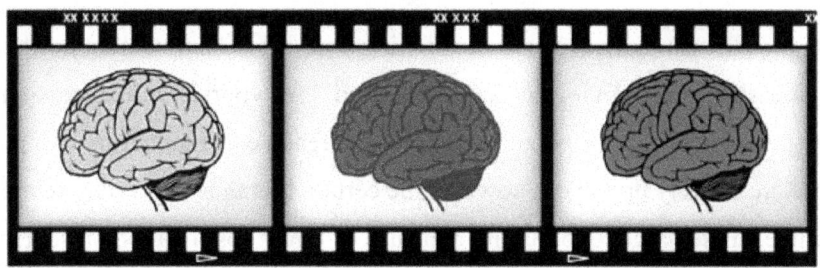

Start your mental movie with yourself in a dangerous environmental setting, perhaps walking through an alley in some dangerous part of the city. Make certain to recreate the whole environment (i.e., sights, sounds, smells, people, time of day, weather conditions, specific buildings or landmarks, etc). For example, feel the frigid night air rush your face. Envision the dilapidated brick buildings menacingly surround you. Allow the stench of urine, vomit and street garbage to assault your nostrils when you walk past the drunken wino. Listen to the sound of cars driving in the distance or hear an alley cat cry from hunger. Remember you need to see everything in vivid detail.

Next, conjure up an ominous figure lurking in the shadows, slowly approaching you. Give him strong physical characteristics. A tall and powerful mesomorph. Begin visualizing his hard and chiseled face and work your way down his massive torso to his thick, oak legs. Smell the stench of bad breath that radiates from his mouth. Give this redoubtable enemy a criminal motive and a deep voice to express it. Feel your heart rate escalate and your adrenaline surges through your veins. Don't forget to visualize critical tactical factors, such as the assailant's range, positioning, and weapon capability.

Visualize a complete reversal in your mentality – the killer side of your soul. Watch yourself transform into an emotionless and vicious combatant. Your mind is razor sharp and focused on the confrontation. Your chest expands as oxygen fills your lungs. Thick veins rise from your temple as your face grins with deadly anticipation. You have hate in your soul and ready to prove it!

Imagine your criminal adversary threatening your life. Then, without hesitation, you unleash a storm of violence and bloodshed. See yourself move inexorably forward with a brutal compound attack. The offensive techniques that you choose are entirely up to you; however, be certain that they accurately relate to the range, angle, target opportunity and "use of force" justification presented by the enemy. Hear the opponent shriek in pain as you dislocate his shoulder. Feel his warm blood splatter on your knuckles as you brutally pummel his face into a bloody mop. Remember to see yourself making all the right moves for the situation at hand.

One of the most important aspects of creative visualization is clarity of your images. For example, make certain your imagined environment is as detailed as this photograph.

To add variety to your visualization scenarios, try:

- Visualizing this scenario at different mental speeds (slow, moderate, fast).
- Experimenting with different real-life combat scenarios.
- Changing the environment.
- Changing the circumstances.
- Changing the type of adversary(s).
- Changing the distance or range of engagement.
- Changing the criminal's motive.
- Changing the criminal's weapon (i.e., knife, gun, bludgeon, etc)
- Be creative and remember that no two self-defense situations (armed and unarmed) are ever the same.

While mental visualization works best for people with vivid imaginations, anyone with the will and desire can master it. Just fifteen minutes of visualization per day will produce significant results. If you find that you have difficulty holding the mental images in your head, consider writing a script of your scenario before you begin.

Some of you might discover that conjuring up a threatening enemy in your mind is difficult. So, to help get you started, I have included a few "bad guys" on the next page that you can add to your personal visualization sessions.

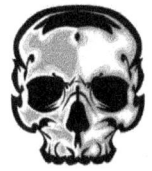

Warning! Be certain that every visualized scenario is legally and morally justified. Never, ever visualize unjustifiable or indiscriminate violence.

The Psycho

The Street Brawler

The Home Invader

The Terrorist

Viciousness

A War Machine is more vicious and ruthless than his enemy. On the battlefield he has a great propensity for extreme violence and destruction. Simply put, he's a savage.

Viciousness is a vital component of mental toughness that can be mentally instilled by pseudospeciating your adversary. Pseudospeciation is the process of assigning inferior or subhuman qualities to your enemy. This psychological tactic is essential because it protects the fighter from the limitations of combat etiquette. It allows the War Machine to fight his enemy with vicious intent and deadly determination by freeing him from the inherent dangers of moral apprehension.

"I have a high art: I hurt with cruelty those who would damage me." -Archilochus

Viciousness should not be misinterpreted as wrong, evil, immoral, or depraved. Some people wonder how the War Machine can reconcile viciousness with virtue. Unfortunately, the concept of viciousness immediately conjures up images of helpless victims being preyed upon by cruel aggressors. But it is this erroneous perception that must be accurately rectified.

The fact is that there are times when viciousness must be met with greater viciousness. Viciousness is an unfortunate but necessary means to achieve and sustain safety, justice, and peace. This may sound paradoxical and extreme. Some may challenge the compatibility of virtue and the capacity for brutal destructiveness. But there is, in fact, no inherent incompatibility. The War Machine must be virtuous and yet altogether capable of unleashing a controlled explosion of viciousness and brutality.

Pseudospeciation is critical in combat because it permits the War Machine to fight his enemy with vicious intent and deadly determination.

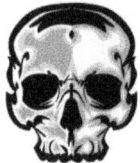 *While viciousness is an essential component of the War Machine psychology, be absolutely certain that your actions are legally and morally justified in the eyes of the law.*

GHOSTING AND PSEUDOSPECIATION

One very effective method of pseudospeciating your adversary during a combat situation is ghosting. Essentially, is the process of mentally eliminating all the facial features on your adversary (particularly his eyes) so that he appears completely faceless. This psychological strategy is important when launching your attack because it will make it psychologically easier for you to attack your adversary with vicious intent and determination.

Ghosting is the process of mentally eliminating all the facial features on your adversary (particularly his eyes) so that he appears completely face-less.

Self-Discipline

The War Machine has an abundant supply of self-discipline. He's in complete control of his mind, which means that he can effectively manage his emotions and desires. This is one of the key traits that separate him from the rest of the masses.

The War Machine consciously fights the tendency toward complacency and comfort. Complacency is an inherent and unfortunate component of humanity that weakens the human spirit. Therefore, the War Machine constantly challenges himself on a daily basis. He is hungry. Always striving for greater heights of achievement.

The War Machine does not follow the path of least resistance. He has tremendous willpower and realizes that hard work pays off in the long run. Delayed gratification is a way of life for him. Resistance to the passing whims and impulses of his mind only raises the War Machine's self-discipline which increases his self-respect. And self-respect is invaluable and priceless!

"In war, discipline is superior to strength." -Publius Flavius Vegetius Renatus

Philosophical Resolution

The War Machine has taken the necessary time to resolve moral issues concerning the use of deadly force in combat. His religious and philosophical beliefs permit him to justifiably take the life of another in battle. As a result, he is free of apprehension and capable of unleashing a maelstrom of violence.

Ironically, your biggest enemy in a combat situation is often your mixed-up moral conscience. For some people, being forced to use deadly force can create apprehension during a life-and-death encounter. This is because of incorrect perceptions or misinterpretation of many religious or associated beliefs.

"On the occasion of every act ask thyself: How is this with respect to me? Shall I repent of it? A little time and I am dead, and all is gone. What more do I seek, if what I am now doing is the work of an intelligent living being, and a social being, and one who is under the same law with God?"-Marcus Aurelius

Our culture and system of government are both based on the Judeo-Christian ethic. With this in mind, our parents, teachers, friends, etc have ingrained morality issues in us. Therefore, such common statements as "pick on someone your own size" or "don't hit a woman" often leave you with the fatal perception that a smaller or female adversary should be treated differently, when, in reality, anyone—regardless of size, age, gender, race, or appearance—has the potential to destroy you. The Bible can also be easily misinterpreted regarding the use of deadly force. This misinterpretation can be identified in two situations.

Hesitation or Failure to Act

The commandment "Thou shalt not kill" can cause people to hesitate to employ lethal techniques. A more accurate translation of this commandment is "Thou shalt not murder" (Exodus 20:13) (murder being the unjustifiable taking of another human life). Some people feel they have no right to kill another human being. When using deadly force, your objective is not to take life from another human being, but to stop your enemy from causing you grievous bodily harm or possible death. However, the possibility of the enemy dying should be of no consequence to you. The bottom line is when warranted and justified, killing another person is permitted even under God's law.

Guilt

People who justifiably employ deadly force later suffer some degree of guilt over their actions. They often question their right to take another life in defense of their own. They believe that life is sacred and that only God has the right to take it away. However, in the Bible, if someone tries to kill another unjustifiably, he forfeits the sanctity of his life, and he suffers any consequences brought on by his own actions (Exodus 21:12 and 14). God commands us to protect our lives from others that would take it away unjustifiably. At the same time, God removes the sanctity of a person who chooses to attempt to take the life of someone else unjustifiably.

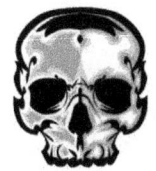 *CAUTION: You must resolve any moral conflicts in your mind prior to placing yourself and others in a situation where deadly force might be employed.*

Responsibility

The War Machine always takes full responsibility for his own actions. He is not one who makes excuses. He's able to make rational decisions on his own and therefore answerable for his own behavior. In battle, the War Machine understands that no one is coming to his rescue. He accepts this fact and fully understands that he's responsible for protecting his life. He knows when he has to be the judge, jury and executioner.

Sadly, we live in a society that is conditioned to expect that someone else will protect us from violence. While the police are there to do the best they can, you cannot rely on them for your own protection and well being. From a practical standpoint, how could anyone expect the police to defend and protect every American citizen all the time? The bottom line is that you and you alone are responsible for protecting and defending yourself and your loved ones.

Unfortunately the War Machine's lethal capability to defend himself carries tremendous moral and social responsibility, as well as the risk of civil liability and criminal jeopardy.

Ironically enough, the more highly trained, knowledgeable, and skilled he is in firearms, knives, and unarmed combat tactics, the higher the standard he must follow when protecting himself and others. If he acts too quickly or uses what others might consider "excessive force" in neutralizing an assailant, he may end up being a defendant in a legal process.

"Zeal to do all that is in one's power is, in truth, a proof of piety." - Flavius Claudius Julianus

If you blind or cripple a person in a self-defense altercation, you'd better be prepared to justify this act in the eyes of the law. If you are not careful, you could spend the rest of your life supporting the person who meant to harm you - assuming, of course, that you can get a job once you get out of jail!

The most popular question self-defense students ask is when can you use physical force. Legally, in order for you to be justified in using force, jeopardy must exist. Keep in mind that there are three elements that constitute jeopardy: ability, opportunity and intent.

Ability - the adversary must have the ability to cause you or another person grievous bodily harm or death (he must have access to something that he can use to cause grievous bodily harm or death).

Opportunity - the adversary must have the opportunity to cause you or another person harm or death (usually involving either proximity or control of their chosen weapon or both); and

Intent - the adversary must have shown a manifested intent to cause you or another person grievous bodily harm or death.

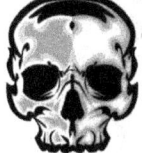 *Being responsible for your self-protection also requires that you have a basic understanding of self-defense and the law. Keep in mind that anytime you use physical force against another person you run the risk of being sued. Be certain that your actions are legally justified.*

PART II
War Machine Physiology

"That which does not kill us makes us stronger."
- Friedrich Nietzsche

Now that you have been introduced to the War Machine's mental component, it's time to look into the physical realm. Looking like a War Machine is not such an easy task. It is a slow and arduous process that will take a considerable amount of time. However, if you are serious about achieving your goal then it can be accomplished.

Appearance Matters!

A War Machine looks imposing. His entire body is forged into a piece of steel that can withstand great physical strain and punishment. His physique is hard, resilient and powerful. Because of his menacing stature and high degree of muscularity, the War Machine often intimidates people. Needless to say, he looks like someone who is not to be reckoned with.

Actually, the War Machine physique serves two objectives. First, it's the ideal vehicle for combat. It permits the warrior to attack and defend with overwhelming strength and power.

Second, it serves as a visual deterrent to any potential criminal assailants. This is what I call **Aesthetic Intimidation.** It's a well-known fact that muggers, street punks, bar room brawlers, rapists, and other members of the underclass look for victims - not challenges. Remember, if you're fat, underweight, or visibly out of shape, you are most likely a walking target for a predatory street criminal.

If you want to be a human War Machine, then you must possess the very same qualities of a heavily armored tank. Essentially, you must be imposing, powerful, mobile and capable of penetrating the enemy's defenses without trepidation. What follows are some visible physical characteristics of a War Machine.

- The face is etched and cheekbones are visible.
- The waistline is firm to the touch.
- The torso has a noticeable V-taper (significant chest-waist differential).

- The entire body is large, shapely and symmetrical.
- Vascularity is prominent in the forearm and arm regions.
- Neck region looks thick and powerful.
- All muscle groups look full and hard.
- Low amount of subcutaneous fat around the body

When it comes to street fighting and hand to hand combat, size and appearance matters! Which one of these individuals are least likely to be attacked in the streets?

War Machine Body Composition Chart

BODY FAT	MENS BODY FAT%	WOMEN'S BODY FAT%
War Machine	Under 11	Under 19
Low (lean)	11 - 14	19 - 22
Average	15 - 17	23 - 27
Fair	18 - 22	28 - 35
Unhealthy	22+	35+

Fighting for your life in today's modern city streets is practically the same as the battling in the Roman colosseum, where the strong would survive and the weak would die!

Weight Training is a Vital Component of This Program!

If you want the appearance of a War Machine then you must train with weights on a regular basis. It's that simple.

I'll be the first one to admit that weight training is not easy work. It's time consuming and uncomfortable at times. Nevertheless, lifting weights serves two major purposes.

One, it's the only effective way of developing and shaping your body into a fearsome physique. Two, it strengthens the body for the tremendous strain of physical combat.

Keep in mind that a scientific weight-training program will also improve the following combat attributes:

- Striking power
- Fighting endurance
- Movement speed
- Improved muscular coordination
- Better body composition
- Higher level of pain tolerance.

There are four general principles that lay the foundation of an effective weight-training program. They are:
- An effective weight-training program must progressively overload your muscles.
- As your muscles become stronger, the resistance must be increased.
- Strength and size gains come quicker from fewer reps and heavy weights.
- Your muscles must be given sufficient time to recuperate from training.

When weight training, be certain to maintain proper form and execute all of your movements in a smooth and controlled fashion. If you are unfamiliar with a particular exercise, don't be apprehensive to ask a certified fitness instructor for assistance.

People sometimes ask if kettlebells can be supplemented for free weight training in the War Machine program. Unfortunately, the answer is no! Kettlebells are a very poor substitute. As a matter of fact, kettlebell training is more of a trendy gimmick that can lead to serious training injuries. Avoid using them!

Combat Utility of Muscles

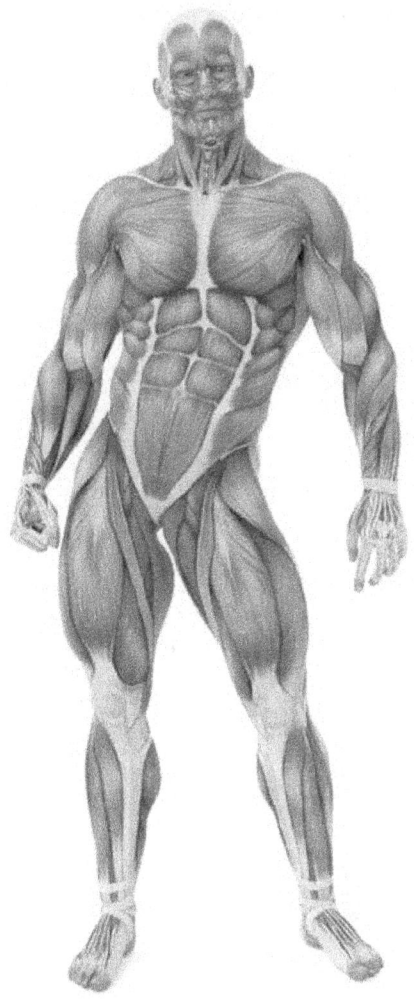

When it comes to unarmed combat performance, muscle mass plays a vital role. The more "functional muscle" you have attached to your body, the better your odds of surviving or winning a fighting situation.

The war machine weight training program is not about getting big and simply looking intimidating to others. If that were the case then every body builder in Venice Beach would be a War Machine. They are far from it!

War Machines look like the combat elite! When it comes to unarmed combat performance, solid muscle mass plays a vital role. Essentially, the more

"functional muscle" you have attached to your bones, the better your odds of surviving or winning a fight. Don't let anyone tell you otherwise.
Weight training significantly improves your ability to fight effectively in a combat situation. Period!

Strong muscles significantly increase the speed and acceleration of both offensive and defensive techniques which assist in maximizing impact power of various strikes. This is often referred to as the "combat utility" of muscle groups.

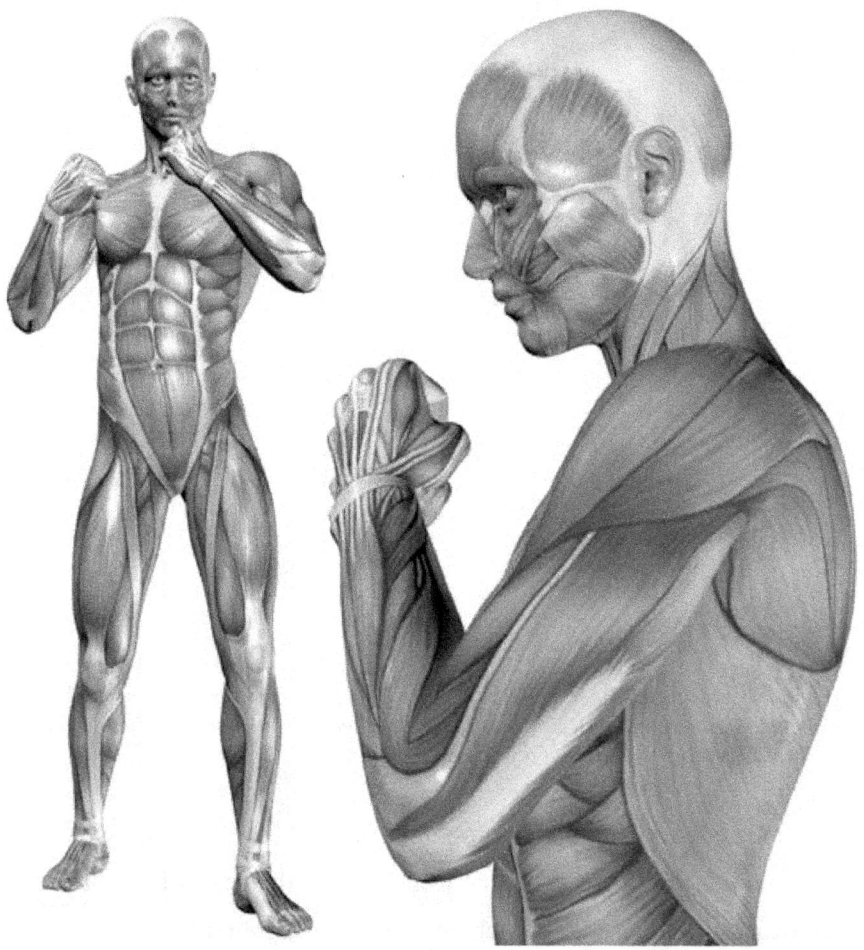

Very few fighters know the actual combat utility of muscle groups. Knowing how each body muscle functions in combat will give you a significant advantage in a real fight

MUSCLE COMBAT UTILITY CHART

MUSCLE GROUP	COMBAT UTILITY
Deltoids	Punching power, blocking solidification, aesthetic intimidation.
Traps	Punching power, aesthetic intimidation.
Neck	Withstand head blows, resistance to chokes, aesthetic intimidation.
Quads	Kicking power, takedown power, ground fighting explosiveness, aesthetic intimidation.
Hamstrings	Kicking power, takedown power, ground fighting explosiveness, aesthetic intimidation.
Forearms	Punching power, blocking solidification, crushing and grappling power, aesthetic intimidation.
Abs	Withstand body blows, ground fighting power, body torque enhancement.
Chest	Grappling and ground fighting power, aesthetic intimidation.
Triceps	Punching power, blocking solidification, aesthetic intimidation.
Calves	Explosive footwork, takedown power, kicking power.
Back	Punching power, grappling and ground fighting strength, aesthetic intimidation.
Biceps	Punching power, blocking solidification, aesthetic intimidation.

Although they might have some similar physical attributes, bodybuilders are not War Machines. As a result, the War Machine program is strictly for combat conditioning and not bodybuilding!

While aesthetic intimidation plays a role in combat, don't always judge a book by it cover. Just because someone appears fit and muscular does not necessarily mean they are formidable in combat. The bottom line is, there are many guys out there who's physiques looks impressive but when push comes to shove, they can't fight their way out of a wet paper bag!

A War Machine might not have the physique of a competitive bodybuilder or fitness model, but I can assure you, he's a wrecking machine in the streets.

The Weight Training Program

Warming-Up & Stretching Out

Prior to lifting weights, it's important that you first warm up and stretch out. Warming up slowly increases the internal temperature of your body while stretching improves your work out performance, keeps you flexible, and helps reduce the possibility of an injury. Some of the best exercises for warming up are jumping jacks, rope skipping or a short jog before training. Another effective method of warming up your muscles is to perform light and easy movements with the weights.

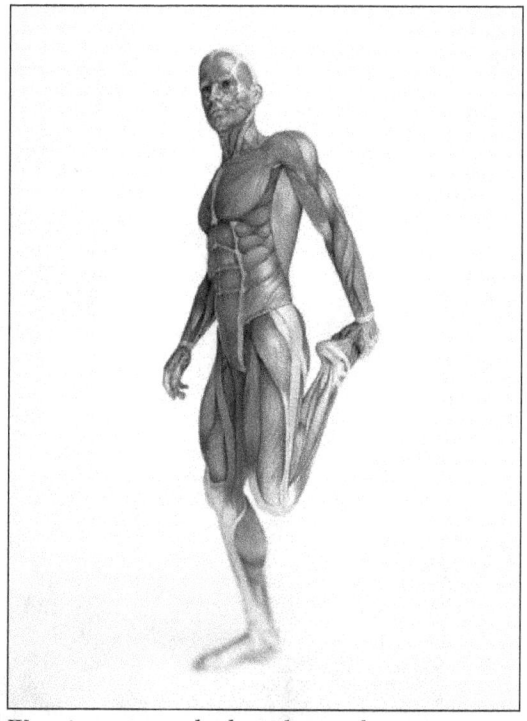

Warming up your body with stretching exercises is imperative to preventing injury.

When stretching out, keep in mind that all movements should be performed in a slow and controlled manner. Try to hold your stretch for a minimum of 60 seconds and avoid any and all bouncing movements. You should feel mild tension on the muscle that is being stretched. Remember to stay relaxed and focus on what you are doing. Here are seven stretches that should be performed.

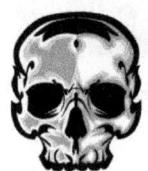

Warning: Before you begin any diet or exercise program, including those suggested in this book, it is important to check with your physician to see if you have any condition that might be aggravated by a reducing diet or strenuous exercise.

Neck stretch - from a comfortable standing position, slowly tilt your head to the right side of your neck, holding it for a count of 20. Then tilt your head to the left side for approximately 20 seconds. Stretch each side of the neck at least three times.

Triceps stretch - from a standing position, keep your knees slightly bent, extend your right arm overhead, hold the elbow of your right arm with your left hand, and slowly pull your right elbow to the left. Keep your hips straight as you stretch your triceps gently for 30 seconds. Repeat this stretch for the other arm.

Hamstring stretch - from a seated position on the floor, extend your right leg in front of you with your toe pointing to the ceiling. Place the sole of your left foot in the inside of your extended leg. Gently lean forward at the hips and stretch out the hamstrings of your right leg. Hold this position for a minimum of 60 seconds. Switch legs and repeat the stretch.

Spinal twist - from a seated position on the floor, extend your right leg in front of you. Raise your left leg and place it to the outside of your right leg. Place your right elbow on the outside of your left thigh. Stabilize your stretch with your elbow and twist your upper body and head to your left side. Breathe naturally and hold this stretch for a minimum of 30 seconds. Switch legs and repeat this stretch for the other side.

Quad stretch - assume a sitting position on the floor with your hamstrings folded and resting on top of your calves. Your toes should be pointed behind you, and your instep should be flush with the ground. Sit comfortably into the stretch and hold for a minimum of 60 seconds.

Prone stretch - lie on the ground with your back to the floor. Exhale as you straighten your arms and legs. Your fingers and toes should be stretching in opposite directions. Hold this stretch for 30 seconds.

Groin stretch - sit on the ground with the soles of your feet touching each other. Grab hold of your feet and slowly pull yourself forward until mild tension is felt in your groin region. Hold this position for a minimum of 60 seconds.

Now that you are warmed up and ready to go, here is a weight training program requiring you to train each muscle group two times per week.

WEIGHT TRAINING PROGRAM

The War Machine weight training program is a three-day split routine where you subdivide your muscle groups over a period of three days so you only have to train four body parts per workout session.

Essentially, you train for two days in a row and then take off one day, then train for two days in a row and take two days off. This weight training routine allows you to train each muscle once every five days.

MON	TUE	WED	THUR	FRI	SAT	SUN
back traps biceps forearm	quads hams calves abs	**REST DAY**	chest deltoids triceps neck	back traps biceps forearm	**REST DAY**	**REST DAY**

You will repeat the following Monday by picking up with Tuesday's workout.

If you have the opportunity to train with free weights, try to use dumbbells whenever the opportunity presents itself. Dumbbells allow for a greater range of motion, they recruit both stabilizer and target muscles, improve neuromuscular coordination, and you can also work around aches and pains more easily.

Unless you have your own gym equipment, your local gym will be your best friend.

Keep in mind the ideal weight-training workout should last somewhere between 45 and 60 minutes. If you cannot complete your daily routine within that period of time then you are not training with the proper amount of intensity. Keep in mind, there are no shortcuts in the War Machine program! The bottom line is you have to lift weights on a consistent basis.

Free weights and machines are all that is needed for the War Machine weight training program. If you don't have such a set up at home you will need to join your local gym.

There is no age limit to the War Machine program. Just make certain you get clearance from your personal physician before you start training.

THE EXERCISES

What follows are the various exercises of the War Machine Program. We will begin with back exercises:

BACK EXERCISES
Lat Pulldowns (front)

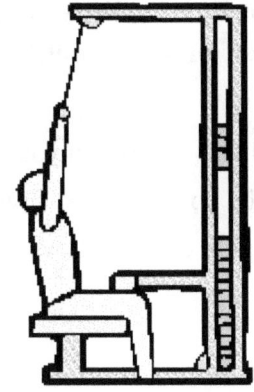

(widens the upper back)
5 sets of 8-10 repetitions

TO PERFORM THE EXERCISE: (1) Grab hold of a lat bar (wide grip) and hook your knees under the pad. (2) Using your upper back, pull the long bar down until it touches the top of your chest. (3) Return back to the starting position.

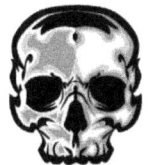

Avoid rounding your back when training your back. Rounding your spine causes your shoulders and arms to do most of the work instead of your back.

T-Bar Rows

(Thickens and strengthens the outer back)
5 sets of 8-10 repetitions

TO PERFORM THE EXERCISE: (1) Position yourself on the T-bar machine with both of your feet flat on the floor plate. (2) Grab hold of the T-bar and slowly lift the weight towards your chest. (3) Lower the weight back to the starting position.

One-Arm Dumbbell Rows

(Strengthens the back)
5 sets of 8-10 repetitions

TO PERFORM THE EXERCISE: (1) Grab hold of a dumbbell, bend forward until your back is parallel to the ground. (2) Support yourself by placing your free hand on the bench. (3) With your palm facing your body, let the dumbbell hang at arm's length. (3) In a controlled manner, lift the weight up to the side of your body. (4) Lower the dumbbell back to the starting position.

One arm rows are great for developing explosive striking techniques. Take your time and build up to the heavy weights.

Deadlifts
(Develops the entire back)
6 sets of 8-10 repetitions

TO PERFORM THE EXERCISE: (1) Grab a barbell with a double overhand grip, making certain your arms are straight and your knees are bent. (2) Keep the barbell close to your legs while making sure to keep your spine neutral. (3) While looking forward, take a deep breath and pull the bar upwards close to your body. (4) Focus on pressing your feet through the floor while simultaneously bringing your chest upwards and moving your hips forward. (5) Next, fully extend your knees and hips and pull your shoulders back (as if standing at attention). (6) To complete the exercise, return the bar back to the ground.

TRAPEZIUS EXERCISES
Barbell Shrugs
(Develops the trapezius)
6 sets of 6-8 repetitions

TO PERFORM THE EXERCISE: (1) With an overhand grip hold a barbell at arms length. (2) In a smooth and controlled fashion, raise your shoulders as high as possible. (3) Hold this position for a moment and then slowly lower it back to the starting position.

You might want to consider using lifting straps when performing shrugs with heavy weights. Lifting straps are inexpensive and can be purchased at most gyms and fitness stores.

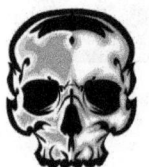

Don't let your ego run your workout program. Always work with a manageable amount of weight and progressively increase the poundages over a period of time.

Dumbbell Shrugs

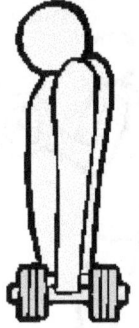

(Develops the trapezius)
4 sets of 6-8 repetitions

TO PERFORM THE EXERCISE: (1) From a standing position and your arms at your sides, hold a dumbbell in each hand. (2) Raise your shoulders as high as possible. (3) Hold for a moment and slowly lower it back to the starting position.

In this photo, the author demonstrates the correct way to perform dumbbell shrugs.

BICEP EXERCISES

Standing Barbell Curls
(Builds mass and strength in the biceps)
4 sets of 8-10 repetitions

TO PERFORM THE EXERCISE: (1) Grab a barbell with your hands-shoulder width apart. (2) With your arms stretched in front of you, curl the bar upward toward your chest. (3) Lower the weight to the starting position. When performing the barbell curls, be certain to keep both of your elbows stationary and close to your body. Avoid the tendency to swing the weight.

When performing barbell curls, keep your form strict.

Preacher Curls

**(Develops and strengthens the lower biceps)
4 sets of 8-10 repetitions**

TO PERFORM THE EXERCISE: (1) Position yourself so your chest is against the preacher bench. (2) Grab hold of a barbell with an underhand grip and curl the bar up towards your face. (3) Lower the weight back to the starting position.

Workout Intensity is another key component of the War Machine program.

Incline Dumbbell Curls
(Develops mass and strength in the biceps)
4 sets of 8-10 repetitions

TO PERFORM THE EXERCISE: (1) Sit in an incline bench (set at approximately 45-degrees) and hold a dumbbell in each hand. (2) Slowly curl the dumbbells up toward your shoulder. (3) Lower the weight back to the starting position.

FOREARM EXERCISES
Barbell Wrist Curls

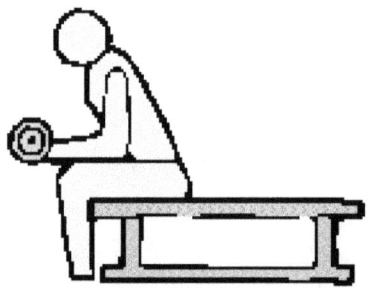

(Builds strength and mass in the flexor muscles)
5 sets of 8-10 repetitions

TO PERFORM THE EXERCISE: (1) Sit at the end of a bench, grab a barbell with an underhand grip and place both of your hands close together. (2) In a smooth and controlled fashion, slowly bend your wrists and lower the barbell toward the floor. (3) Contract your forearms and curl the weight back to the starting position.

Hammer Curls

(Builds strength in the forearms)
5 sets of 6-8 repetitions

TO PERFORM THE EXERCISE: (1) Stand with both feet approximately shoulder width apart, with both dumbbells at your sides. (2) Keeping your elbows close to your body and your palms facing inward, slowly curl both dumbbells upward towards your shoulders.

All forearm exercise can also be performed with dumbbells. It will just require a bit more coordination to perform the movements. Be patient with it and you will perfect the movements in no time at all.

Behind-the-Back Wrist Curls
(Builds strength and mass in the flexor muscles)
5 sets of 6-8 repetitions

TO PERFORM THE EXERCISE: (1) Hold a barbell behind your back at arm's length (your hands should be approximately shoulder-width apart). (2) Uncurl your finger and let the barbell slowly roll down your palms. (3) Close your hands and roll the barbell back into your hands.

Reverse Wrist Curls
(Develops and strengthens the extensor muscles)
6 sets of 6-8 repetitions

TO PERFORM THE EXERCISE: (1) Sit at the end of a bench, hold a barbell with an overhand grip (your hands should be approximately 11 inches apart) and place your forearms on top of your thighs. (2) Slowly lower the barbell as far as your wrists will allow. (3) Flex your wrists upward back to the starting position.

QUADRICEPS EXERCISES
Squats

(Builds mass and strength in the thighs)
5 sets of 8-10 repetitions

TO PERFORM THE EXERCISE: (1) With you feet approximately shoulder width apart and in front of your hips, rest a barbell across the back of your shoulders while holding it in place with both hands. (2) While keeping your head up, back straight and your feet flush against the floor, slowly bend your knees and lower your body until your thighs are parallel to the ground. (3) Push yourself back to the starting position.

It's important to always use a weight lifting belt when performing heavy squatting.

Leg Press

(Builds mass and strength in the thighs)
5 sets of 8-10 repetitions

TO PERFORM THE EXERCISE: (1) Position yourself in a leg press machine with both feet close to each other. (2) Bend both of your knees and slowly lower the weight to your chest. (3) Press the weight back to the starting position.

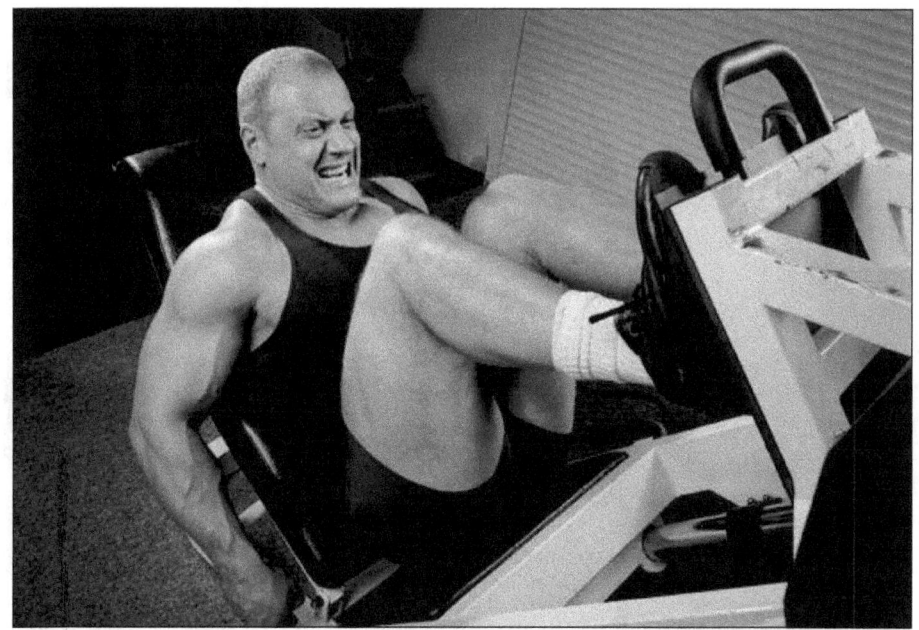

Unlike squats, the leg press does not require a great deal of coordination or balance to perform.

Leg Extensions

(Shapes and strengthens the thighs)
5 sets of 8-12 repetitions

TO PERFORM THE EXERCISE: (1) Position yourself in the leg extension machine with both of your feet under the padded bar. (2) In a slow and controlled fashion, extend both of your legs as far as possible until they have reached the lockout position. (3) Return the weight slowly to the starting position.

HAMSTRING EXERCISES
Leg Curls

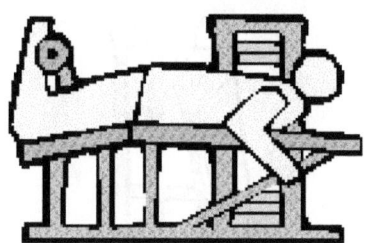

(Builds strength and size in the rear of thigh)
6 sets of 8-10 repetitions

TO PERFORM THE EXERCISE: (1) Lie face down on a leg curl machine, hold onto the handles and place you heels under the padded bar. (2) While keeping your stomach flat on the bench, slowly curl your legs up as far as possible. (3) Slowly lower the weight to the starting position.

Straight-Leg Deadlift

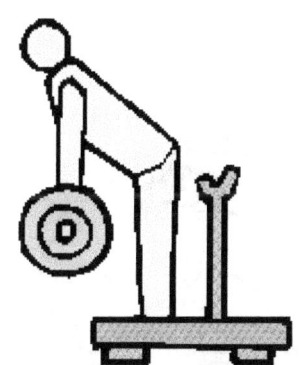

(develops the rear of thigh)
4 sets of 8-10 repetitions

TO PERFORM THE EXERCISE: (1) Grab hold of a barbell while maintaining a standing position. (2) While keeping both of your legs straight, bend forward at your waist until your back is parallel to the ground. (3) Slowly return to the starting position.

CALF EXERCISES

Standing Calf Raises

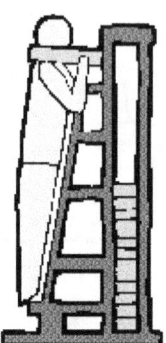

(Builds mass and strength in the calves)
6 sets of 8-10 repetitions

TO PERFORM THE EXERCISE: (1) Stand in front of a calf raise machine with your toes at the end of the footplate. (2) With your shoulders under the pads and your back straight, lower your heels as far as possible to the ground. (3) Now, lift the weight up as far as possible. (4) Slowly return to the starting position.

Seated Calf Raises

(Develops and strengthens the calves)
6 sets of 8-10 repetitions

TO PERFORM THE EXERCISE: (1) Sit in the calf raise machine and place both of your feet on the bottom of the floor plate. (2) In a smooth and controlled manner, lower both of your heels as far as possible. (3) Press upward with your toes. (4) Return back to the starting position.

Calf development is critical to explosive footwork. Powerful calves will allow you to propel your body through the ranges of unarmed combat with ease. Do not neglect this important body part!

Calf development is one of the most overlooked muscle groups. Strong calf muscles are vital for explosive footwork skills.

ABDOMINAL EXERCISES
Decline Crunches

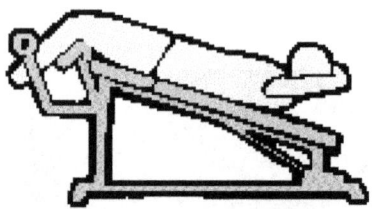

(Strengthens the upper abdominal region)
5 sets until muscular failure is achieved

TO PERFORM THE EXERCISE: (1) Place both your feet under the pads of the decline bench and cross your arms over your chest. (2) In a smooth and controlled fashion, slowly lift your upper body to approximately 45-degrees from the bench. (3) Then slowly lower your torso until it touches the bench.

Hanging Knee Raise

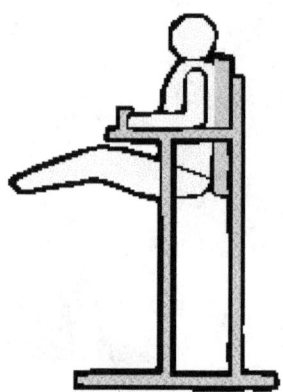

(Strengthens the lower abdominal region)
5 sets until muscular failure is achieved

TO PERFORM THE EXERCISE: (1) Hang from a chin-up bar with your hands shoulder-width apart. (2) With your knees bent, use your abs and lift your knees into your chest. (3) Hold this position for a second and then slowly lower yourself to the starting position.

If you are one of those people who can perform countless repetitions when performing abdominal exercises, consider adding weight to induce muscular failure. Always start out with light weight and slowly increase the poundage.

Your "core" is actually comprised of many different muscles that cover the entire length of your torso which stabilize your spine and pelvis and which provide a solid foundation for movement. Strong abdominal muscles help keep your back healthy, hold your body upright, improves your balance and significantly enhances your combat skills and techniques.

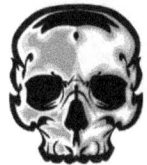 ***WARNING!** When performing crunching movements, avoid interlocking your fingers behind your head. This lessens the effectiveness of the exercise and places tremendous strain on your cervical vertebrae. To remedy this, simply cup your hands behind your ears and lift your torso with your abdomen.*

CHEST EXERCISES

Bench Press

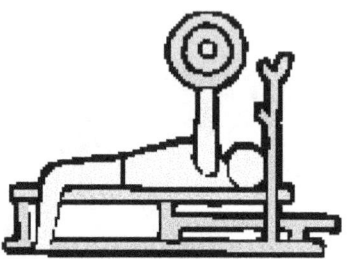

(Builds mass and strength in the chest region)
5 sets of 8-10 repetitions

TO PERFORM THE EXERCISE: (1) Lie on a flat bench with both of your feet flat on the floor. (2) Grab hold of the barbell (your grip should be slightly wider than shoulder width), lift it off the rack and slowly lower it until it touches slightly below your chest area. (3) Press the bar upward to the starting position. Note: The bench press is a standard mass building exercise for the chest. It produces size, strength in the chest as well as the front of the shoulders. Make it a regular component of your chest routine. You will be glad you did!

The bench press can also be performed with dumbbells.

Incline Bench Press

**(Builds mass and strength in the upper chest region)
5 sets of 8-10 repetitions**

TO PERFORM THE EXERCISE: (1) Lie on an incline bench with both of your feet flat on the floor. (2) Grab hold of the barbell with your grip slightly wider than shoulder width. (3) Lower the weight down to the upper chest area and press it back to the starting position.

Dumbbell Flys
**(Builds mass and strength in the chest region)
5 sets of 8-10 repetitions**

TO PERFORM THE EXERCISE: (1) Lie on a flat bench with both of your feet flat on the floor. (2) Hold two dumbbells above you and slowly lower the weight outwards in a wide and controlled arc (your arms should be slightly bent). (3) Lift them back up (along the same arc) to the starting position.

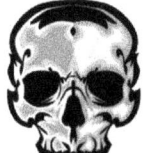 *Never lockout your arms when performing the dumbbell flys, as this can can cause serious damage to your elbows. Always maintain a slight bent-arm position during the movement.*

The mind body connection is an essential component of the War Machine program. Always remain focused on what you are doing through the course of your entire workout.

DELTOID EXERCISES
Seated Military Press

(Develops the front of the shoulders)
5 sets of 8-10 repetitions

TO PERFORM THE EXERCISE: (1) From the seated position, hold the barbell at shoulder height. (2) While keeping your back straight, press it straight up to the top and then lower it to the starting position.

Standing Lateral Raises

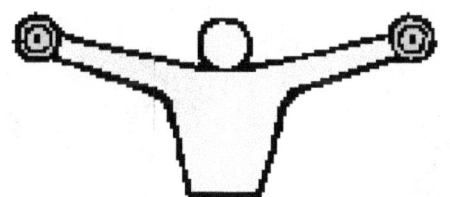

(Develops the sides of the shoulders)
4 sets of 8-10 repetitions

TO PERFORM THE EXERCISE: (1) Hold the dumbbells at your waist and bend forward slightly. (2) Raise both dumbbells to your side until they reach approximately shoulder height. (3) Slowly lower them to the starting position

If you don't have lower back problems, the military dumbbell press can also be performed while standing.

Seated Bent-Over Raises
(Develops the rear portion of the shoulders)
4 sets of 8-10 repetitions

TO PERFORM THE EXERCISE: (1) Sit at the end of a bench, legs together with a dumbbell in each hand. (2) Bend forward at your waist, with both arms slightly bent raise the weights up until your arms are parallel to the floor. (3) Slowly lower them to the starting position.

TRICEP EXERCISES
Cable Pressdowns

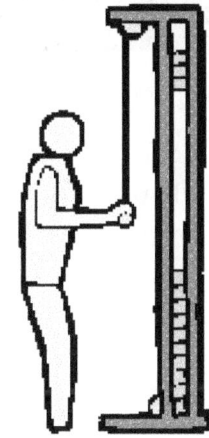

(Builds mass and strength in the triceps)
4 sets of 8-10 repetitions

TO PERFORM THE EXERCISE: (1) Stand in front of an overhead cable and pulley. (2) Grasp the short bar with an overhand grip with your hands approximately 11 inches apart. (3) With your elbows close to your sides and your body straight, press the bar down as far as possible. (4) Slowly return the bar to the starting position.

When performing triceps pressdowns, avoid the tendency to lean forward as this works your shoulder muscles.

Bench Dips

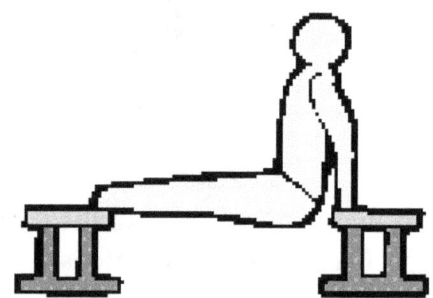

(Builds thickness and strength in the triceps)
4 sets of 8-10 repetitions

TO PERFORM THE EXERCISE: (1) Position a bench behind your back and place your hands at the edge approximately shoulder-width apart. (2) Then place both of your heels on another bench. (3) Slowly bend both of your elbows and lower your body to the floor. (4) Push yourself back up to the starting position.

Lying Dumbbell Extensions
(Builds strength in the outer triceps)
4 sets of 8-10 repetitions

TO PERFORM THE EXERCISE: (1) Lie on a flat bench with both feet flat on the floor. (2) Hold two dumbbells overhead (both of your palms should be facing each other). (3) While holding your elbows in place, slowly lower the dumbbells to the sides of your head until both of your triceps are completely stretched. (4) Press the dumbbells back up to the starting position.

NECK EXERCISES

Neck Bridges
(Develops the neck muscles)
4 sets of 10-12 repetitions

TO PERFORM THE EXERCISE: (1) Lie on your back with your head touching the floor. (2) With your hands stabilizing your body, arch your back and roll onto the top of your head. (3) Return to the starting position.

Neck Lifts
(Develops the neck muscles)
5 sets of 6-8 repetitions

TO PERFORM THE EXERCISE: (1) Sit in a chair with the neck harness on your head and the weight plate between your legs. (2) Slowly pull your head upwards as far as possible. (3) Return to the starting position.

You will need a neck harness to perform the neck lifts. Most leather harnesses can be purchased through mail order. Check the various fitness magazines or specialty catalogs for more information on this product.

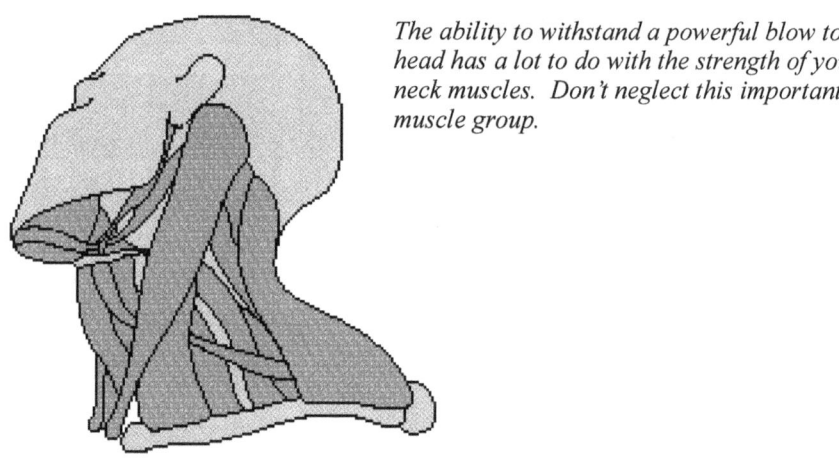

The ability to withstand a powerful blow to the head has a lot to do with the strength of your neck muscles. Don't neglect this important muscle group.

Strengthen Your Hands!

Don't neglect strengthening your hands and fingers. Strong fingers and hands are important for tearing, crushing, and gouging techniques, as well as improving the structural integrity of your fists.

There are many efficient ways of strengthening your hands, wrists and forearms for the rigors of hand to hand combat. If you are low on cash and just starting out, you can begin by squeezing a tennis ball a couple times per week. One hundred repetitions per hand would be a good start.

Later on you can add power putty to your strengthening routine. This unique hand exerciser is made up of silicone rubber that can be squeezed, pulled, pinched, clawed and stretched in just about any conceivable direction. This tough resistant putty will strengthen the muscles of you forearm, wrists, hands and fingers.

The simple action of firmly gripping a barbell or dumbbell can help improve your hand and forearm strength.

Another quick and effective way to strengthen your hands, wrists and forearms is to work out with heavy duty hand grippers. While there are a wide selection of them on the market, I personally prefer using the Captains of Crush brand. These high quality grippers are virtually indestructible and they come in eleven different resistance levels ranging from 60 to 365 pounds. Finally, you can also condition your wrists and forearms by performing the various free weights forearm exercises discussed in this book.

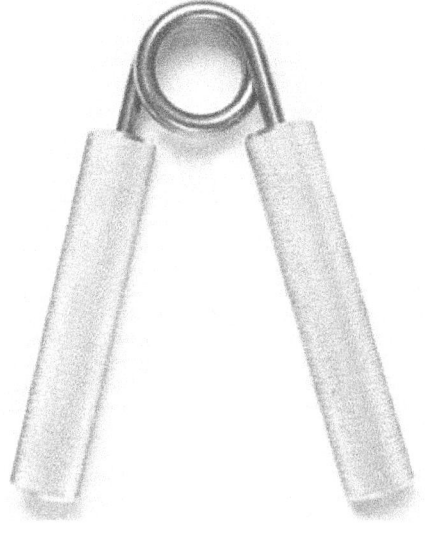

Without a doubt, Captains of Crush brand, make the best hand grippers on the market.

Running - The Ultimate Conditioner

Running is a significant part of the War Machine program. Not only will it get you in top physical condition, but running will also improve your wind capacity, endurance, circulation, and muscle tone.

Remember to start your running sessions with a brisk jog, working up to a faster pace. Always start off slowly and progressively build up speed.

The War Machine program requires you to run a minimum of four times per week for a duration of approximately 60 minutes. Later you can consider adding hill or step running to your training routine. Try to get into the habit of running in the morning hours. The air is cleaner and during the hot summer months it is usually cooler.

Running style is another important consideration. Avoid stomping on the ground. Try running lightly and rhythmically with your arms and shoulders relaxed. Let your feet glide across the floor. Running should be practically silent. In fact, if you hear your feet hit the ground you'll know that your running incorrectly. Every running session should include the following stages: warm-up; main workout; cool down; and stretches. And always try to buy the best running shoes that you can afford. Your feet will thank you later.

A treadmill is great when weather conditions prevent you from running outdoors. If your finances permit, invest in a quality treadmill.

A Word about Training Partners

Training partners are good. Especially when weight training, a good work out partner should motivate, challenge and push you to your limits. When lifting heavy weights, a training partner can watch over you and force out those extra important repetitions. When it comes to equipment training, you'll also need a partner to hold and manipulate the focus mitts, striking shield, kicking cylinder, etc.

While a good training partner can be a major asset, having a bad one can be a major liability. Be exceptionally careful about who you choose to train with you.

Caution! Some injuries are often caused by the following: lifting too much weight too soon, unsound lifting mechanics, improper hand or foot placement when working with machines, your training partner isn't paying attention, or the free-weight plates slides off the bar during the exercise.

A good training partner is invaluable and can push you through tough workouts.

Be alert when working out! Some injures are often caused by the following: lifting too much weight too soon, unsound lifting mechanics, improper hand or foot placement when working with machines, your training partner is not paying attention, or the free-weight plates slides off the bar during the exercise.

PAIN - The Necessary Evil

Since pain is a natural residual of being a War Machine, it's important to understand it and know how to overcome its debilitating effects. To begin, there are two types of pain: growth pain and injury pain.

Growth pain is usually experienced when training and working out. For example, when lifting weights you might experience a dull burning sensation in the belly of your muscles. This type of fatigue-related pain is actually good and you should push through it.

The second type of pain is called injury pain. Again, in the example of weight lifting, if you experienced a sharp and intense pain in a particular joint this might indicate damage to either a tendon, ligament or muscle. This is your body warning you to stop the exercise immediately. Obviously, pushing through injury pain is counter productive and stupid.

Ironically enough, injury pain can also be an ally that informs you of immediate danger in a combat situation. For example, when your adversary lands a lucky blow to your body. In such a situation, the pain receptors in your torso will immediately alert you to the damage, allowing you to adapt accordingly to the situation.

Pain Tolerance

A War Machine can tolerate a tremendous amount of pain. He knows it's a necessary evil that must be harnessed and controlled if he is to grow in the gym or prevail in a combative altercation.

To begin, it's very important that you change your perceptions of pain and ultimately recognize it as an unavoidable element of combat. Once you can accept this fact, you will be one step closer to controlling it and lessening its deleterious effects. Generally speaking, the fighter who can tolerate a higher degree of pain is more likely to win the fight than a combatant with a lower pain tolerance.

If you are one of the many people who have a difficult time managing pain (growth and injury), here are some training techniques that have proven to be helpful.

Stay Relaxed - One of the best methods of controlling pain (growth or injury) is to stay relaxed and avoid tensing your body. Not only will relaxation ease the pain and help control your breathing, it will put you in a better physiological state to counter attack your opponent during a fight.

Positive Mind Set - What you are thinking can greatly affect the way you act. A negative mind-set can lead to feelings of fear, apprehension, failure and despair and an increase in pain. However, a positive mind-set promotes relaxation, confidence, success and pain reduction.

Positive Self-Talk - Another method of pain tolerance is positive self-talk. Positive self-talk means talking to and convincing yourself to work through the pain. It requires that you mentally talk to yourself in a positive manner.

Impact Training - Impact training is a series of physical exercises that condition you to withstand pain. In unarmed combat, there are two types of striking impact: snapping and breaking.

Snapping impact shocks the head or body but does not fully penetrate it. It's quick but lacks substantial follow-through. A snapping blow usually makes a brisk, sharp cracking sound when it connects with its target.

In contrast, breaking impact shocks and moves the head or body. It can break or fracture bones easily because it follows through its target (approximately three inches). You must be physically and psychologically prepared to tolerate both types of impact.

Impact training requires both forms of impact to be administered to specific body parts, including:

- Shoulders
- Back
- Chest
- Biceps
- Triceps
- Abdominals
- Thighs
- Calves

Never strike the head or face when conducting impact training.

For impact training, your training partner will need a pair of boxing gloves or focus mitts to deliver the blows. When you begin, have your partner start off slowly with light strikes to your muscle groups. Have your partner alternate snapping and breaking blows. Always remember to exhale when the blow makes contact. Over time, your partner can increase the speed and force of the strikes. Be patient with each other. It will take time and some experimentation before you and your partner can properly gauge the amount of force. Impact training sessions should last approximately five minutes and should be conducted at least twice a month.

WARNING: Never strike the face, neck, throat, solar plexus, spine, groin, or joints during impact training. These anatomical targets are very sensitive and cannot be conditioned to withstand deliberate impact. Striking these targets can cause severe and permanent injury. It is imperative that your training partner delivers accurate blows and avoids these targets during training.

Since we spend most of our lives trying to avoid pain, it will require a considerable amount of time to condition yourself not to instinctively withdraw from anything that hurts.

Rest and Burnout

The war machine program is very taxing on both the mind and body. It is no surprise that rest is an essential component of combat conditioning training. Training intensely day after day will lead to either burnout (overtraining) and/or injury. The simple fact is your body needs time to recoup and replenish itself from grueling workouts.

Burnout is simply defined as a negative emotional state acquired by physically overtraining. Some symptoms of burnout include physical illness, fatigue, poor training performance, anxiety, disinterest in training, and general sluggish behavior.

By following the following suggested tips, you can help avoid the deleterious effects of burn out.

Here are a few suggestions to help avoid burnout in the war machine program:
1. Make your workouts intense but enjoyable.
2. Stagger the intensity of your workouts.
3. Work out while listening to different types of music.
4. Pace yourself during your workouts—don't try to do it all in one day.
5. Listen to your body—if you don't feel up to working out skip a day.
6. Work out in different types of environments.
7. Use different types of training equipment.
8. Work out with different training partners.
9. Keep accurate records of your training routine.
10. Vary the intensity of your training throughout your workout.
11. Daily monitor your mental and physical energy levels.

While there are many methods in preventing burnout, one very effective rule of thumb is to take off two days per month and two weeks per year. Remember that growth occurs when you rest - not when you work!

Nutrition & Supplements

Diet and nutrition are also important aspect of the war machine program. In reality, a true diet refers to a life-style of eating right.

To begin, 55 percent of his daily caloric intake should consist of complex carbohydrates. Carbohydrates, the body's primary source of energy, are found in vegetables, fruits, potatoes, pasta, and all grain products.

Next we have proteins, which are essential for muscle and tissue growth. Poultry, fish, and legumes are excellent sources of low-fat proteins. Since you are involved in the war machine program, you will require a greater amount of protein than the average person. Generally speaking, you should consume 1-1.5 grams of protein per pound of lean mass.

Finally, unsaturated fats are vital to proper metabolic function and vitamin absorption and should make up 10 percent of your calories. Don't confuse unsaturated fats with their nasty relatives, saturated fats. Saturated fats, found in ice cream, chocolate, cakes, and so on, are a big NO! Forget them. They will only make you fat and sluggish. Look for natural unsaturated fats in such foods as nuts, seeds, and various grains.

Despite what some might say, not all carbohydrates are not bad for you. Just remember to consume them in moderation.

Do not forget to drink plenty of water throughout the day. Water is essential nutrient and it plays a significant role in all bodily processes. When following the war machine program, try to drink at least one gallon of water per day!

Vitamins

Nutritional supplements should also be taken to ensure that you are receiving all the necessary vitamins and minerals within your diet. A vitamin is any of various fat-soluble (stored in the body fat) or water-soluble (dissolve in water) organic substances essential for the growth and maintenance of the body.

Vitamins are a necessary part of the war machine's diet. While a well-balanced diet will ensure that you are taking in the necessary amounts of vitamins, deficiencies can still occur, and they can have a negative effect on your training and overall performance. Be certain to get the following vitamins within your daily diet.

Vitamin A - this fat-soluble vitamin is important for normal cell growth and development. Vitamin A can be found in fish-liver oils, carrots, liver, fortified dairy products, and some yellow and dark green vegetables.

Vitamin D - this fat-soluble vitamin helps build healthy bones and teeth, and it can be obtained from fortified milk, fish, and eggs, and by exposing your body to sunlight.

Before you put anything into your mouth, get into the habit of always reading its nutritional information

Vitamin E - this fat-soluble vitamin is used to treat abnormalities of the muscles, red blood cells, liver, and brain. This vitamin can be found in seed oils, especially wheat germ oil, plant leaves, and milk.

Vitamin K - this fat-soluble vitamin is important for blood clotting and preventing hemorrhaging. It can be found in fish oils, liver, egg yolks, tomatoes, and green, leafy vegetables.

Vitamin B1 (Thiamin) - this water-soluble vitamin functions as a coenzyme and is necessary for carbohydrate metabolism and neural activity. Thiamin can be found in meat, yeast, and the bran coat of grains.

Vitamin B2 (Riboflavin) - is the primary growth-promoting factor in the vitamin B complex. It can be found in milk, leafy vegetables, liver, nuts, brewer's yeast, meat, and egg yolks.

Niacin - a component of the vitamin B complex used to treat and prevent pellagra (a disease that includes skin eruptions, nausea, vomiting, nervous system disturbances, and mental deterioration). Niacin can be found in meat, fish, poultry, wheat germ, dairy products, and yeast.

For those who follow a very intense weight training routine, I strongly suggest taking some type of vitamin and mineral mega pack. Essentially, mega-packs provide large or "mega" doses of necessary vitamins and minerals. that can help active and promote anabolic benefits.

Vitamin C (Ascorbic Acid) - this water-soluble vitamin prevents scurvy and a variety of dental problems. Vitamin C can be found in citrus fruits, tomatoes, turnips, sweet potatoes, potatoes, and leafy green vegetables.

Did you know that it is practically impossible to get all the nutrients that your body needs from food alone. A multi-vitamin is your nutritional insurance.

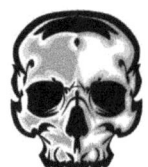 *Warning: Avoid excessive amounts of fat-soluble vitamins, because they can cause severe toxicity.*

Death of Champions!

Anabolic steroids are synthetic chemical compounds that resemble the male sex hormone called testosterone. This "performance-enhancing" drug is widely known to increase lean muscle mass, strength and endurance in most athletes. Steroids also help muscles recover rapidly from strenuous workouts. Most anabolic steroids are taken in pill form, however some are taken by injection. Many users will cycle steroids (taking the drugs for 6 to 12 weeks then stopping for a period of time and then starting again).

Anabolic Steroids

Anabolic steroids produce terrible side effects and therefore should not be incorporated into the war machine program. Short-term use of such drugs can be extremely harmful, even fatal. Here's a list of some possible side effects:

- Liver damage or cancer
- High blood pressure
- Reduction of "good" cholesterol
- Gastrointestinal disorders
- Headaches and nosebleeds
- Gagging and vomiting
- Jaundice
- Baldness

- Gynecomastia (development of breast like tissue in males)
- Impotence
- Acne
- Bad breath
- Increased chance of tendon, ligament, and muscle injury
- Violent and homicidal mood swings known as "Roid Rages"
- Severe depression
- Muscle cramps and spasms

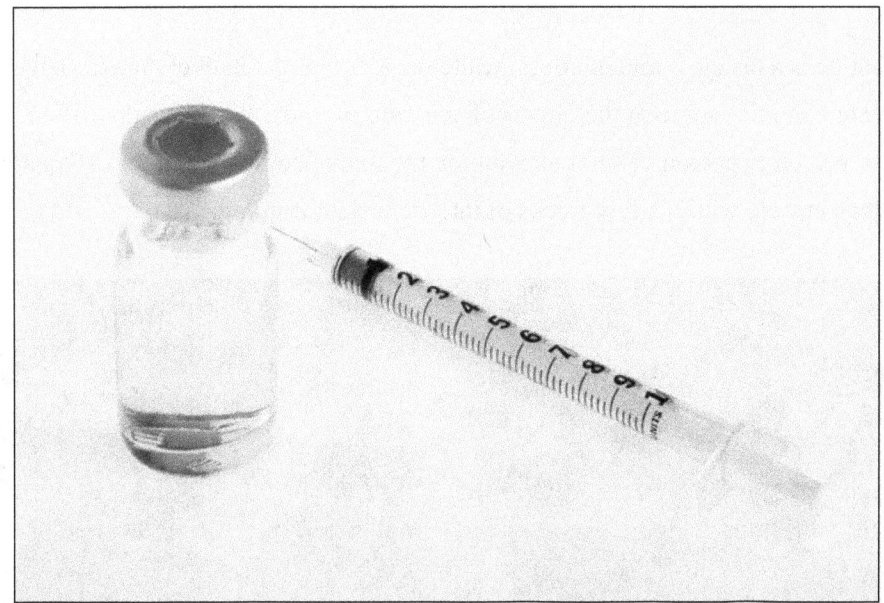

Unless there is a specific medical reason, steroids should be avoided all costs.

Supplements - What you really need!

If you look at any bodybuilding magazine you will see literally hundreds of advertisements for supplements claiming to make you bigger and stronger in the shortest amount of time. With so much stuff on the market, it's hard to choose the best supplements for your combat conditioning program.

Throughout the years, I have discovered three supplements that are tried and true for gaining lean muscle mass and strength. They include: creatine, glutamine and whey protein. Let take a look at each one.

Creatine

One safe alternative to anabolic steroids is creatine. Creatine is a fascinating supplement that can benefit anyone who wants to boost their strength and endurance and build lean muscle mass.

Creatine is a tasteless and odorless, white powder that is relatively inexpensive. Creatine mimics some of the effects of anabolic steroids. While results will vary from person to person, it's not uncommon for some people to gain 5 to 10 pounds of lean muscle within a few weeks of intense weight training.

WARNING! *Always consult with your doctor before taking Creatine Monohydrate or any other training supplement.*

The best time to consume creatine is approximately 1/2 hour before weight training and then right after a workout. Also, be certain to drink plenty of water when taking creatine (at least eight-8 ounce glasses per day). Creatine needs water for cell volumization of the muscle.

Be careful when purchasing creatine. There are some manufacturers who sell impure creatine that can be harmful to your body. Make certain you are ingesting 100% pure creatine. Demand to see the HPLC (high-performance liquid chromatography) test results from whomever you purchased your creatine from. If you purchase creatine that has a strange smell or is yellow in color, return it immediately to the place of purchase and get a full refund.

Glutamine

Next, is Glutamine. Essentially, glutamine is an amino acid produced in the body that plays a vital role in protein synthesis. Despite its abundance in the muscles, glutamine levels can become quickly depleted when your body undergoes intense training. As a matter of fact, it has been stated that it can take up to approximately six days for Glutamine levels to return to normal after intense weight training sessions.

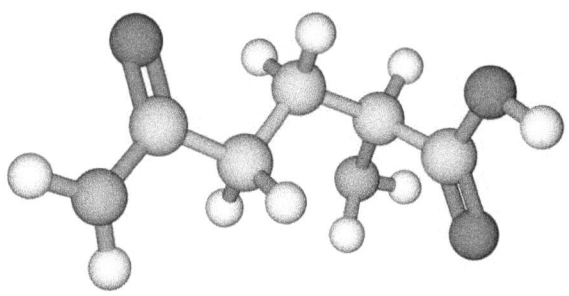

Illustration of a glutamine molecule.

While dosages can often vary from person to person, most people should take 5 grams. It has also been stated that the best time to take glutamine is right before you go to sleep.

BENEFITS OF GLUTAMINE
Aids in protein synthesis
Promotes cell volumizing
Helps prevent muscle breakdown
Helps secrete Human Growth Hormone

Whey Protein

Whey is a high quality protein that is loaded with all the essential amino acids. The benefit to whey protein is that it is rapidly digested and helps quickly repair your muscles following intense training.

As you can imagine, there are numerous brands of whey protein sold on the market at various prices. The good news is whey protein tastes decent and comes in a wide range of flavors, so you will most likely find something that agrees with your palette.

How Much Protein?

There is much debate on the subject of protein consumption for combat conditioning, muscular development and overall health. Generally speaking, the average healthy adult male following the War Machine program should consume approximately 1-1.5 grams of protein per pound of body weight. For example, a 175 pound man would consume anywhere from 175 to 262 grams of protein per day. This 1-1.5 protein ratio will help with the following:

- Build muscle mass
- Maintain muscle tone while losing fat
- Increase strength
- Improving combat performance

The good news is whey protein is available in a wide variety of delicious flavors.

If you don't have time to make a protein shake, there are dozens of protein bars available at grocery and convenient stores. Just be certain to read the nutritional content before making a purchase, as some of these "bars" are extremely high in calories and fat.

As a general rule of thumb, the best time to ingest whey protein is within 30 - 45 minutes of working out. This is known as the "post workout-anabolic" window.

Other Good Protein Sources
Grass-Fed Beef
Organic Chicken
Wild Salmon
Tuna fish
Tilapia
Tempeh
Quinoa
Almonds and Almond Butter
Pumpkin/squash seeds
Black walnuts
Egg whites
Cottage cheese 2% low fat
Hemp seeds
Pistachios
Organic, (Greek) Yogurt

PART III
War Machine Combatives

"The bravest are surely those who have the clearest vision of what is before them, glory and danger alike, and yet notwithstanding go out to meet it. -Thucydides

There are several preliminary concepts that a War Machine must understand and ultimately master before his fighting techniques can be effectively applied in battle. They are: range proficiency, stances of combat, strategic positioning, footwork, the balance of forces, target awareness, combat attributes, strike first, switching to auto pilot, the killer instinct, and weapon's check. Let's begin with range proficiency.

Range Proficiency
Combat is unfair and unpredictable. It can occur anytime and anywhere. If you want to be victorious in a street fight then you'd better be range proficient. Range proficiency is ability to fight your adversary in all three distances of unarmed combat (kicking range, punching range, grappling range). Let's take a closer look at each distance of unarmed combat.

Kicking Range
The furthest distance of unarmed combat is kicking range. At this distance you are usually too far away to strike with your hands, so you would use your legs to strike your opponent. Kicking range tools can be safe, economical and powerful if they are delivered to targets below the opponent's waist.

The kicking range of unarmed combat.

105

Punching Range

Punching range is the mid-range of unarmed combat. At this distance, you are close enough to the enemy to strike him with your hands and fists. Punching range tools are quick, efficient and effective. They are the foundation of your compound attack arsenal.

The punching range of unarmed combat.

Grappling Range

The third and closest range of unarmed combat is grappling range. At this distance, you are too close to your opponent to kick or execute some hand strikes, so you would use close-quarter tools and techniques to neutralize your adversary.

Grappling range is divided into two different planes, vertical and horizontal. In the vertical plane, you would deliver impact techniques, some of which include elbow and knee strikes, head butts, gouging and crushing tactics, and biting and tearing techniques. In the horizontal plane, you are ground fighting with your enemy and can deliver all of the previously mentioned techniques, including various submission holds, locks, and chokes.

The Neutral Zone

In unarmed combat, the neutral zone is not a range of combative engagement. It is the distance at which neither you or your opponent can physically strike one another. The neutral zone enhances your defensive reaction time and is therefore the ideal place to be when assessing your environment and your adversary.

RANGE	CHARACTERISTICS
KICKING	Requires minimal commitment with the assailant, provides enhanced defensive reaction time, considered a telegraphic range, non-neutralization range, permits distance gap closing techniques, safest initiation range.
PUNCHING	Preferred range of combat in CFA, offers reduced defensive reaction time, considered a neutralization range, facilitates efficient technique deployment, relatively non-telegraphic range, requires moderate commitment with your assailant.
GRAPPLING	Considered a neutralization range, non-telegraphic range, requires maximal commitment with the assailant, dangerous and least preferred range of unarmed combat, most common range of engagement.

There are numerous advantages and disadvantages to the various ranges of unarmed fighting. Knowing the strategic and tactical characteristics of these ranges can give you a substantial advantage in a combat situation.

Stances of Combat

A trained combatant will never stand squarely in front of his enemy. If the opportunity presents itself, he will always assume a strategic stance. Combat stances are crucial in battle because it minimize target exposure, enhance balance, promote mobility and significantly increases striking power.

In order to be prepared for all forms of combat, you need to master a broad scope of strategic stances. They include: the fighting stance, natural stance, deescalation stance (punching and kicking ranges), deescalation stance (grappling range), first strike stances, knife defense, bludgeon defense stance, knife fighting stance and stick fighting stance.

The Fighting Stance

The fighting stance is an aggressive posture that a war machine assumes when squared off with his enemy. In unarmed combat, the fighting stance is used for both offensive and defensive purposes. It stresses strategic soundness and simplicity over complexity and style. The fighting stance also facilitates maximum execution of body weapons while simultaneously protecting your vital anatomical body targets against possible counterstrikes.

When assuming a fighting stance, blade your feet and body at 45-degrees from your assailant. This moves your body targets back and away from direct strikes but still leaves you strategically positioned. Keep your stronger side forward, facing your adversary. Place your feet approximately shoulder-width apart. Keep both knees bent and flexible. Keep both of your hands up and align your lead hand in front of the rear. When holding up your

In this photo, the author demonstrates the left lead fighting stance.

guard, make certain not to tighten your shoulders or arms. Stay relaxed and loose. Finally, keep your chin slightly angled down.

Simply learning how to use a fighting stance is not enough to win a fight. You will also need to remember to stick to the fundamental. For example, always keep both of your hands up when fighting with your opponent. Avoid the natural tendency to lower your hands when fighting. This will leave you wide open to a possible counter attack in a hand to hand combat situation. Remember, when executing a punch or strike to always keep your other hand up to either defend against a counter strike or follow up with another strike. One of the best ways to train yourself to keep your hands up when fighting is through simulated street fighting, full contact sparring sessions and punching bag workouts.

Natural Stance

The natural stance is used when approached by an individual (i.e., drunken bum, street vagrant, etc.) who appears nonthreatening, yet suspicious. To assume this stance, angle your body 45- degrees from the suspicious individual and keep both of your feet approximately shoulder-width apart. Your knees should be slightly bent with your weight evenly distributed. Keep both of your hands in front of your body with some type of natural movement (e.g., rub your hands together, scratch your wrist, or scratch your temple), which will help protect your upper targets from a possible attack. Do remember to stay relaxed but alert, avoiding any muscular tension in your shoulders, neck, or arms

De-escalation Stance (kicking & punching ranges)

The De-escalation stance is used when diffusing a hostile person. The proper de-escalation stance (for kicking & punching ranges) can be acquired first blading your body at approximately 45- degrees from the adversary. Then keep both of your feet approximately shoulder-width apart and have your knees slightly bent with your weight evenly distributed. Both of your hands are open, relaxed, and up to protect the upper targets of your centerline. Keep your torso, pelvis, head, and back erect and stay relaxed and alert—while remaining at ease and in total control of your emotions and body. Remember to avoid any muscular tension—don't tighten up your shoulders, neck, arms, or thighs (tension restricts breathing and quick evasive movement, and it will quickly sap your vital energy).

De-escalation Stance (grappling range)

The De-escalation stance for grappling range is accomplished by first blading your body at approximately 45-degrees from the adversary. Then keep both of your feet approximately shoulder-width apart, knees slightly bent, and your weight evenly distributed. Place both of you hands side-by-side with your hands open, relaxed, and up to protect the upper gates of your centerline.

The de-escalation stance in the kicking and punching range of unarmed combat.

It's important to keep your torso, pelvis, head, and back erect. Stay relaxed and alert while remaining at ease. Once again the key is avoid any muscular tension - don't tighten up your shoulders, neck, arms or thighs

First Strike Stance

The first strike stance (kicking & punching range) is used prior to initiating a first strike in a fight. It facilitates "invisible deployment" of a preemptive strike while simultaneously protecting your vital targets against various possible counter attacks.

When assuming the first strike stance, have both of your feet approximately shoulder-width apart, knees slightly bent with your body weight evenly distributed over each leg. Blade your body at a 45-degree angle from your adversary. This position will help situate your centerline at a protective angle from your opponent, enhance your balance, promote mobility and set up your first strike weapons. Next, make certain to keep your torso, pelvis, head and back straight. And always stay relaxed and ready. Do not make the mistake of tensing your neck, shoulders, arms or thighs. This muscular tension will most certainly throw off your timing, retard the speed of your movements and telegraph your intentions.

The grappling range de-escalation stance.

Your hand positioning is another critical component of the first strike stance. When confronted with an opponent in the kicking and punching ranges of unarmed combat, keep both of your hands open, relaxed and up to protect the upper gates of your centerline. Both of your palms should be facing the opponent with your lead arm bent between 90 and 120 degrees while your rear arm should be approximately 8 inches from your chin. When faced with an opponent in grappling range, keep both of your hands side by side of one another.

Knife Defense Stance

Defending against an edged-weapon attack requires mastery of the knife-defense stance. This protective stance will ensure maximal mobility and minimal target exposure, while simultaneously facilitating immediate counterstrike ability.

To assume the knife defense stance, first angle your body (internal organs) approximately 45 degrees from your enemy. Second, slightly hunch your shoulders forward and let your stomach sink in while keeping your head and face back and away from random slashes or stabs. Third, keep your hands, forearms, and elbows close to your body to diminish target opportunities for your assailant.

Remember to cup your hands with your palms facing you, which will turn soft tissue, veins, and arteries in the arms away from the blade. Also keep your knees slightly bent and flexible with your feet shoulder-width apart, and your weight equally distributed on each leg.

The knife defense stance.

Bludgeon Defense Stance

When unarmed and faced with a bludgeon (baseball bat, heavy club, 2X4, etc.) attack, the bludgeon defense stance is your safest bet.

To assume this stance, keep your body angled approximately 45-degrees from the attacker with both of your arms raised to the sides of your head. Keep your torso slightly crouched with your arms and elbows close to your head and body. As with all the combat stances, keep your knees slightly bent and flexible with your feet shoulder-width apart, and your weight equally distributed on each leg. Remember that mobility is a vital component of defending against a bludgeon attack.

Knife Fighting Stance

The knife-fighting stance is used when both you and the enemy are armed with knives or edged weapons. When assuming this combat stance, keep you feet about

The bludgeon defense stance.

shoulder-width apart, body angled at approximately 45-degrees from the adversary and both of your knees bent with your body weight equally distributed over both legs. This will permit quick footwork, which is so vital for effective knife fighting. Next, keep your torso slightly crouched with your head angled down and your arms and elbows close to your body. Your lead (strong) hand holds the knife close to your body with the cutting edge facing down.

Always hold your knife in your front hand when knife fighting. This knife-forward stance is critical because it brings your closest weapon (your knife) to the assailant's closest targets and the unprotected (or unarmed) side of your body is kept back and away from your opponent's stabs and slashes.

Avoid overextending your knife hand when knife fighting. This is dangerous because it inhibits your balance, leaves you vulnerable to attack, and it significantly reduces your ability to attack your enemy. The only time your knife should leave your body is when you're executing an attack.

Stick Fighting Stance

In this stance, stand with your feet about shoulder-width apart, body angled at approximately 45-degrees from the adversary and both knees bent with the body weight equally distributed over each leg. The torso is slightly crouched with the head angled down and the arms close to the body. Your lead (strong) hand holds the stick close to the body with the weak hand ready for use.

The knife fighting stance.

While a stance is an essential component of combat, there might be some situations that will not afford you the luxury of assuming any type of stance. Always be prepared to deploy your fighting techniques without any foundational structure.

Stance Selection for Combat

Stance selection is the ability to select the appropriate stance for a particular self defense situation. Effective stance selection requires you to understand and instinctively master all of the stances of combat. Bear in mind that the longer it takes for you to select the correct stance for the situation, the greater your chances of serious injury or possible death in a self defense altercation.

Strategic Positioning

Strategic positioning means acquiring the most advantageous position against the adversary. In the event you are overwhelmed by an **assault**, the standard tactical principle is for you to move to a strategically safe position. There are several factors to consider when attempting to acquire a strategic position in combat. They are: live side, dead side, inside position and stance angulation.

The Live Side

When your adversary is squared off in a combat stance, his "**live side**" is the side of his body that is furthest away to you. For example, if your adversary is standing in a right stance (also know as a southpaw stance), his left side is considered the *live side*. In this hypothetical situation, the "live side" would be a relatively unsafe direction to move towards because you're moving into his rear appendages (i.e., rear cross, rear leg kicks, etc).

The Dead Side

When your adversary is squared off in a stance, his "**dead side**" is the side of his body that is closest to you. For example, if your opponent is standing in a right stance, his right side is considered the dead side. In this case, the opponent's right side or "dead side" would be the safest direction to move toward because it's the farthest away from the assailant's rear appendages.

The Inside Position

One of the most dangerous areas of your assailant is his inside position. The inside position is the area between both of his arms where he has the greatest amount of control. From a defensive perspective, the opponent's inside position (the area between both of his arms) is very dangerous because this is where he has the greatest amount of control, leverage and power and also where he can launch his offensive strikes with relative ease. When defending against your opponent's offensive techniques, try to maneuver yourself outside of the opponent's inside position.

The inside position is the area between both of the enemy's arms. From a defensive perspective, this is the most dangerous area on your adversary. It is where he has the greatest amount of control.

Stance Angulation

When squared off with an adversary, your lead leg is positioned in between your assailant's legs. This will permit maximum offensive deployability of your tools and techniques.

Footwork

If a War Machine is to eliminate his enemy swiftly, then he must be mobile. Mobility is defined as the ability to move the body quickly and economically, this can be accomplished through basic footwork. Safe footwork requires quick economical steps performed on the balls of the feet, while relaxed and balanced.

The Basics

Basic footwork can be used for both offensive and defensive purposes, and it is structured around four general directions: advancing, retreating, sidestepping right and sidestepping left.

1. Moving forward (advancing). From your fighting stance, first move your front foot forward (approximately 24 inches) and then move your rear foot an equal distance.

2. Moving backward (retreating). From your fighting stance, first move your rear foot backward (approximately 24 inches) and then move your front foot an equal distance.

3. Moving right (sidestepping right). From a fighting stance, first move your right foot to the right (approximately 24 inches) and then move your left foot an equal distance.

4. Moving left (sidestepping left). From a fighting stance, first move your left foot to the left (approximately 24 inches) and then move your left foot an equal distance. Note: Practice these four movements everyday in front of a full-length mirror until your footwork is quick, balanced, and natural.

Advanced Footwork

Once you have mastered basic footwork, you can then incorporate strategic circling to his repertoire of skills. Strategic circling is an advanced form of footwork where a fighter uses his lead leg as a pivot point. This advanced footwork can be used defensively to evade an overwhelming assault or offensively to strike the enemy from various strategic angles. Strategic circling can be performed from either a right or left stance.

Circling right (from a right stance). From a right lead stance, step 8 to 12 inches to the right with your right foot, then use your right leg as a pivot point and wheel your entire rear leg to the right until the correct stance and positioning is acquired. Remember to keep both of your hands up.

Circling left (from a left stance). From a left lead stance, step 8 to 12 inches to the left with your left foot, then use your left leg as a pivot point and wheel your entire rear leg to the left until the correct stance and positioning is acquired.

The Balance of Forces

The War Machine is a paradigm of both balance and power. He's knows how to maintain his equilibrium when fighting his enemy. Balance is critical because it permits quick and efficient movement, prevents unnecessary target exposure and it allows quick recovery from committed movements. Moreover, losing your balance in combat can often result in losing your life.

If you want to avoid losing your balance in a fight, strive to maintain proper body mechanics when executing both your offensive and defensive techniques. Also, avoid excessive follow-through when throwing punches and always keep your center of gravity directly under your body.

Anatomical Targets

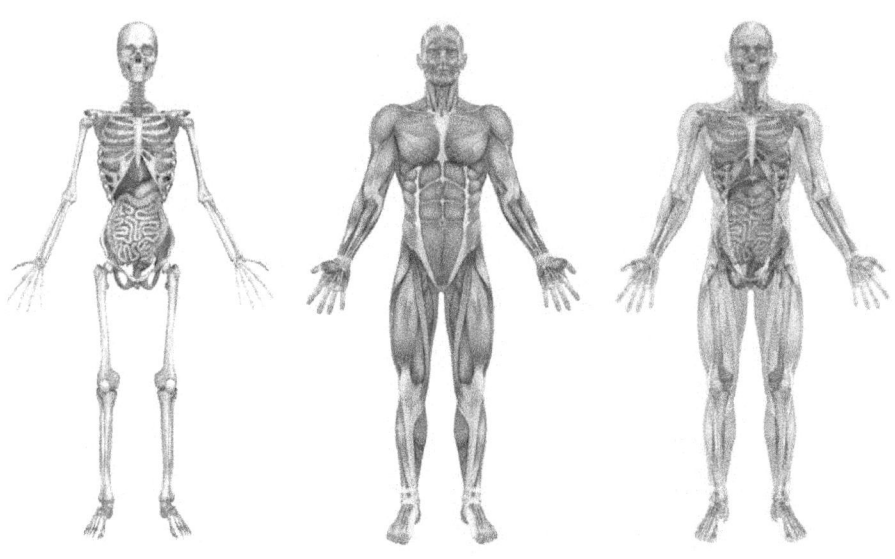

Target Awareness

A skilled fighter knows *what, where, when and how* to strike his adversary. This is known as "target awareness". Simply put, target awareness is a culmination of five strategic principles. They are: target orientation, target recognition, target selection, target impaction and target exploitation. Lets take a look at each one.

5 Components of Target Awareness
Target Orientation
Target Recognition
Target Selection
Target Impaction
Target Exploitation

Target Orientation

Target orientation means having a workable knowledge of the various anatomical targets presented in both armed and unarmed combat encounters.

Target orientation is actually divided into five different categories. They include the following:

- **Impact Targets** - anatomical targets that can be struck with your natural body weapons.
- **Non-Impact Targets** - anatomical targets that can be strangled, twisted, torn, crushed, clawed, gouged, or strategically manipulated.
- **Edged Weapon Targets** - anatomical targets that can be punctured or slashed with a knife or edged weapon.
- **Bludgeon Targets** - anatomical targets that can be struck with a stick or bludgeon.
- **Ballistic Targets** - anatomical targets that can be shot by a firearm.
- **Chemical Irritant Targets** - anatomical targets that can be exposed to by chemical irritants.

For the purposes of this book, I will just address target orientation specifically for unarmed combat. Therefore, we only need to concern ourselves with impact and non impact anatomical targets.

Target Zones

Essentially, there are 13 **anatomical striking targets** that can be found in one of three possible target zones. They are:

Zone One (head region) consists of targets related to the assailant's senses, including the eyes, temples, nose, chin, and back of neck.

Zone Two (neck, torso, and groin) consists of targets related to the assailant's breathing, including the throat, solar plexus, ribs, and groin.

Zone Three (legs and feet) consists of anatomical targets related to the assailant's mobility, including the thighs, knees, shins, and instep/toes.

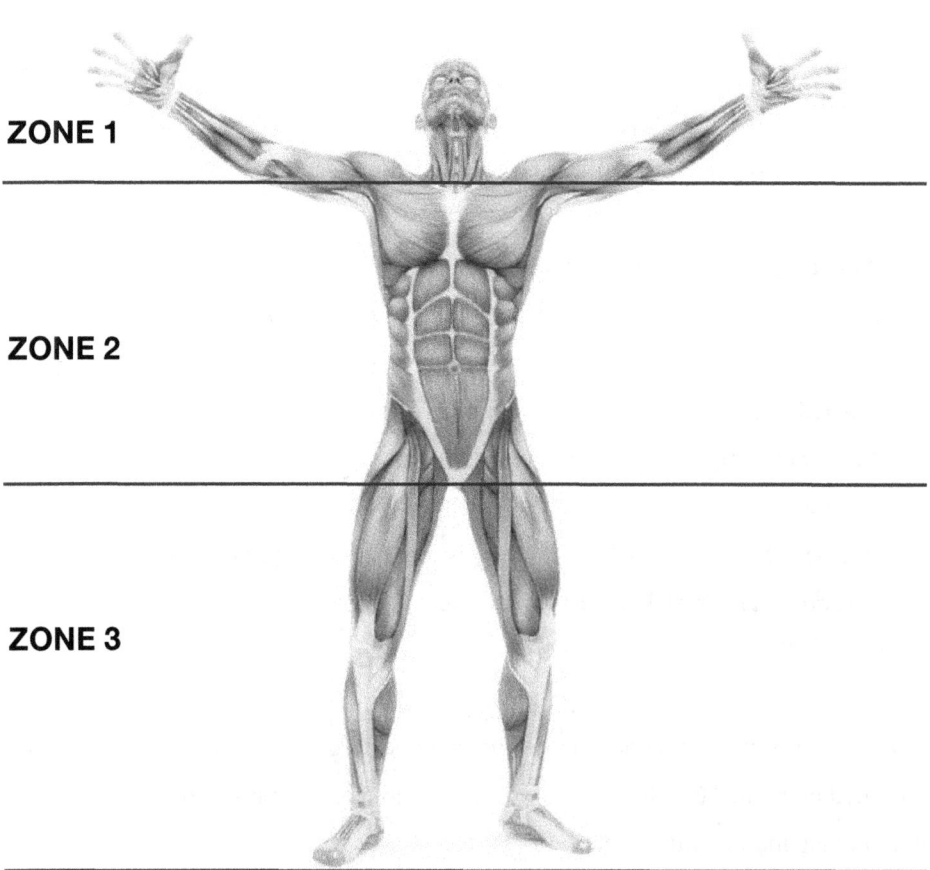

Simply knowing the specific locations of various anatomical targets is not enough. Target orientation also requires that you have a strong understanding of the medical implications of striking these targets. As a matter of fact, every martial artists or combat specialist has the moral and legal responsibility to know the medical implications of each and every offensive strike and technique. A competent combatant must know exactly which anatomical targets will stun, incapacitate, disfigure, maim, or kill his adversary. Therefore, let's take a closer look at these targets and the medical implications of each.

EYES: The eyes are ideal targets for street fighting because they are extremely sensitive and difficult to protect. The eyes can be poked, scratched, and gouged from a variety of angles and vantages. Depending on the force of your strike, it can cause numerous injuries, including watering of the eyes, hemorrhaging, blurred vision, temporary or permanent blindness, severe pain, rupture, shock, and even unconsciousness.

TEMPLES: The temple or sphenoid bone is a thin, weak bone located on both sides of the skull approximately one inch from the assailant's eye. Because of its inherently weak structure and close proximity to the brain, a very powerful strike to this anatomical target can be deadly. Other possible injuries include unconsciousness, hemorrhaging, concussion, shock, and coma.

NOSE: The nose is made up of a thin bone, cartilage, numerous blood vessels, and many nerves. It is a particularly good impact target because it stands out from the assailant's face and can be struck in three different directions (up, straight, down). A moderate blow can cause stunning pain, eye-watering, temporary blindness, and hemorrhaging. A powerful strike can result in shock and unconsciousness.

CHIN: The chin is also a good target for unarmed street combat. When the chin is struck at a 45-degree angle, shock waves are transmitted to the cerebellum and cerebral hemispheres of the brain, resulting in paralysis and immediate unconsciousness. Depending on the force of your blow, other possible injuries include broken jaw, concussion, and whiplash to the assailant's neck.

BACK OF NECK: The back of the assailant's neck consists of the first seven vertebrae of the spinal column. They function as a circuit board for nerve impulses from the brain to the body. The back of the neck is a lethal target because the vertebrae are poorly protected. A very powerful strike to the back of the assailant's neck can cause shock, unconsciousness, a broken neck, complete paralysis, coma, and death.

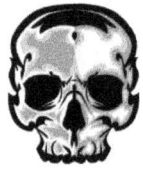

Warning: The temple, back of neck and throat are classified as lethal impact targets that should only be attacked when deadly force in warranted and justified in the eyes of the law.

THROAT: The throat is considered a lethal target because it is only protected by a thin layer of skin. This region consists of the thyroid, hyaline, cricoid cartilage, trachea, and larynx. The trachea, or windpipe, is a cartilaginous cylindrical tube that measures four and a half inches in length and approximately one inch in diameter. A direct and powerful strike to this target may result in unconsciousness, blood drowning, massive hemorrhaging, strangulation, and death. If the thyroid cartilage is crushed, hemorrhaging will occur, the windpipe will quickly swell shut, and the assailant will die of suffocation.

RIBS: There are 12 pair of ribs in the human body. Excluding the 11th and 12th ribs, they are long and slender bones that are joined by the vertebral column in the back and the sternum and costal cartilage in the front. Since there are no 11th and 12th ribs (floating ribs) in the front, you should direct your strikes to the 9th and 10th ribs.

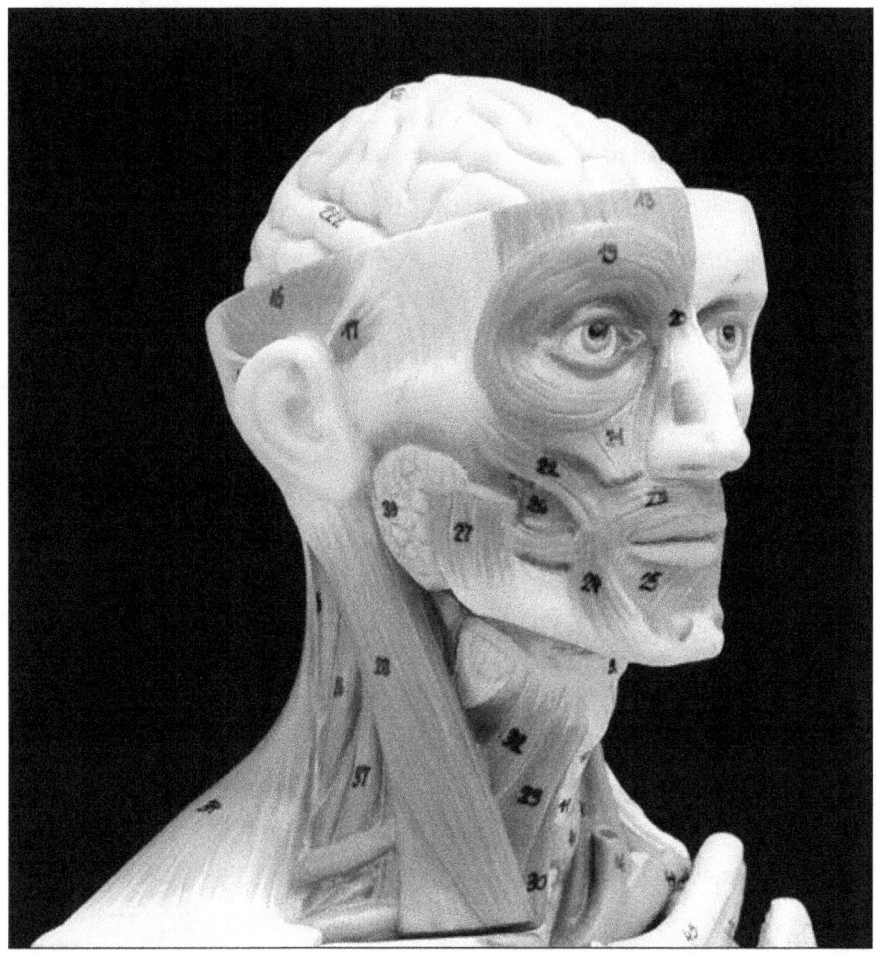
While there are 13 striking targets on the enemy, the assailant's head region is the War Machines primary target.

A moderate strike to the anterior region of the ribs may cause severe pain and shortness of breath. An extremely powerful 45-degree blow could break the assailant's rib and force it into a lung, resulting in the lung's collapse, internal hemorrhaging, air starvation, unconsciousness, excruciating pain, and possible death.

SOLAR PLEXUS: The solar plexus is a large collection of nerves situated below the sternum in the upper abdomen. A moderate blow to this area can cause nausea, pain, and shock, making it difficult for the adversary to breathe properly.

A powerful strike to the solar plexus can result in severe abdominal pain and cramping, air starvation, and shock.

GROIN: The testes can be kicked, punched, or crushed. A moderate kick or strike to an assailant's groin can cause a variety of possible reactions, including severe pain, nausea, vomiting, shortness of breath, and possible sterility. A powerful strike to the groin may crush the scrotum and the testes against the pubic bones, causing shock and unconsciousness.

THIGHS: Since the thighs are large and difficult to protect they make excellent striking targets in a fight. Although you can kick the thighs at a variety of different angles, the ideal location is the assailant's common peroneal nerve located on the side of the thigh, approximately four inches above the knee. Striking this area can result in extreme pain and immediate immobility of the afflicted leg. An extremely hard kick to the thigh may result in a fracture of the femur, internal bleeding, severe pain, intense cramping, and long-term immobility.

KNEES: The knees are relatively weak joints that are held together by a number of supporting ligaments. When the assailant's leg is locked or fixed in position and a forceful strike is delivered to the front of the joint, the crucial ligaments will tear, resulting in excruciating pain, swelling, and immobility. Located on the front of the knee joint is the kneecap, or patella, which is made of a small, loose piece of bone. The patella is also vulnerable to possible dislocation by a direct, forceful kick. Severe pain, swelling, and immobility may also result.

SHINS: The shins are also very sensitive targets because they are only protected by a thin layer of skin. A powerful kick delivered to this target may fracture it easily, resulting in extreme pain, hemorrhaging, and immobility of the afflicted leg.

FINGERS: The fingers are exceptionally weak and vulnerable. They can easily be jammed, sprained, broken, torn, and bitten. While a broken finger might not stop a determined fighter, it will certainly force him to release his hold. A broken finger will also make it very difficult for the assailant to clench his fist or hold a knife or bludgeon. When attempting to break the fingers, it's best to grab the finger securely and then forcefully tear backward against the knuckle.

TOES: In grappling range, a powerful stomp of your heel can break the small bones of the assailant's toes, causing severe pain and immediate immobility. Stomping on the assailant's toes is also one of the best ways for releasing many holds. Keep in mind that you should avoid attacking the toes if the attacker is wearing hard leather boots (e.g., combat, hiking, or motorcycle boots).

Which Biological System to Attack?

As most of you know, the human body is made up of various biological or "organ systems" that must work together to sustain life. For example, human anatomy includes the digestive system, muscular system, nervous system, skeletal system, respiratory system, circulatory system as well as several others.

However, if you have been paying close attention you should have discovered that when it comes to delivering striking techniques (during unarmed combat) we only need to concern ourselves with the

Despite what some martial art instructors say, the human muscular system provides no targets opportunities for unarmed combat. Striking the enemy's chest, arms and shoulder will yield poor results and should be completely avoided.

following three systems. They include:

- **The Skeletal system (bones/joints)**
- **The Nervous system (brain/nerves)**
- **The Respiratory system (lungs)**

Despite what some martial art instructors say, the human muscular system is not a viable system to attack in unarmed combat. For example, striking the enemy's chest, arms and shoulder will yield poor results and should be completely avoided.

Target Recognition

Target recognition is the ability to immediately recognize specific anatomical targets prior to or during a street fight. The following natural body weapon targets are located on your adversary: the eyes, temple, nose, chin, back of neck, front of neck, solar plexus, ribs, groin, thighs, knees, and shins.

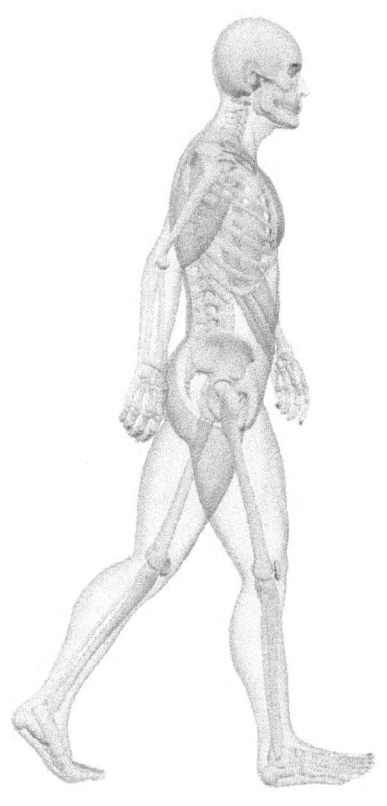

The human skeletal system offers much more target opportunities in unarmed combat. Striking and destroying the enemy's skeletal system produces immediate results in a fight.

Target recognition requires that you maintain a complete visual picture of your adversary (i.e., head, torso and limbs). One of the biggest mistakes that you can make during a street fight is to gaze or stare into your opponent's eyes. Looking steadily into the assailant's eyes will significantly restricts your ability to recognize targets during a fight.

Target Selection

A War Machine will never strike his enemy with reckless abandon. His swift blows are strategically calculated and he is a true maven of target selection. Target selection is the cognitive process of selecting the appropriate anatomical target to attack in combat. Selecting the appropriate target to strike is predicated on three important factors:

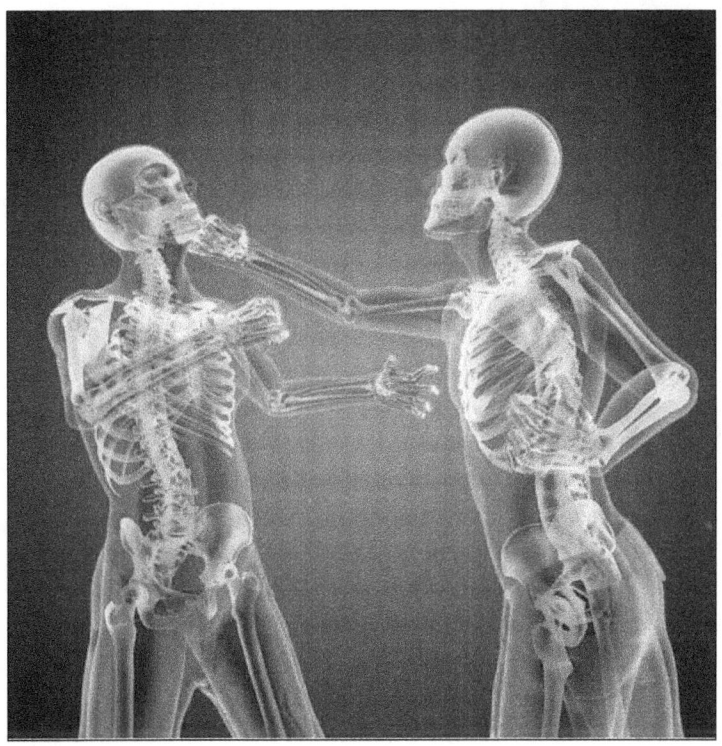

A skilled fighter should practically have x-ray vision. He must be able to see through his opponent's flesh and locate the vulnerable impact

FACTOR 1: Proximity of Opponent - how far the opponent is from your natural body weapon, technique, or weapon.

FACTOR 2: Positioning of Opponent - exactly where is the opponent positioned and at what angle and height.

FACTOR 3: Use of Force - the amount of force (non-deadly or deadly) that is legally warranted for this particular self-defense situation.

Target Impaction

Target impaction is the physical process of successfully striking the selected anatomical target. Target impaction requires that each and every blow be delivered with maximum speed and power and minimal telegraphing. Proper attribute development will ensure successful target impaction during the course of a street fight.

Target Exploitation

Finally, once you have acquired target selection, you can implement target exploitation. Target exploitation is a combative attribute that allows you to strategically maximize (through exploitation) your assailant's **reaction dynamics** during the fight. By the way, target exploitation skills can also be applied in both armed and unarmed encounters.

Attributes of Combat

If you want to prevail in a combat situation must possess a wide range of combat attributes. Combat attributes are unique qualities that enhance or amplify a particular tool, technique or skill set. In the War Machine Program, combat attributes are divided into one of two categories:

- Cognitive attributes
- Physical attributes

Cognitive attributes are the mental properties that enhance your fighting skills and abilities. Some examples include: courageousness, perceptiveness, viciousness, decisiveness, awareness and the killer instinct.

Physical attributes are the physical qualities that enhance your street fighting skills and abilities. They might include: speed, power, timing, agility, ambidexterity, weapon and technique mastery and combat conditioning.

While the War Machine possesses over one hundred combat attributes, there are seven qualities, which are especially important for street combat. They are:

- Speed
- Impact power
- Ambidexterity
- Offensive timing
- Balance
- Non-telegraphic movement
- Relaxation

Speed

In both armed and unarmed fighting you have to be fast- real fast! Your offensive and defensive techniques must move like a flash of lightening.

Actually, combat speed is a chief fighting attribute necessary for both reality based self defense and combat sports training. What most people don't realize is fighting speed is something that you can easily improve. There are specific drills and exercises or "speed training" that can dramatically boost the quickness of your punches, kicks, blocks and other fighting moves.

Combat speed is much like a steel chain made up of several separate links that are related to one another. Each link in the combat speed chain represents a particular component or unique attribute of quickness that must be practiced to maximize the overall acceleration of your martial arts skills and abilities.

The Five Speed Links

The five combat speed links include the following:
- Visual reflex speed
- Tactile reflex speed
- Recognition reflex speed
- Auditory reflex speed
- Core movement speed

If all five speed links are developed and combined in a speed training workout, you will notice a big improvement in all of your fighting skills. These improvements will include:

• Rapid punching combinations will help you overwhelm your opponent both in the streets or the ring.

• Swifter kicking means less technique telegraphing and greater impact power.

• Improved offensive timing leads to better target accuracy and maximum impact power.

• Improved defensive timing improves blocking, parrying and evasion movements.

• Explosive footwork permits you to close the distance gap between you and your opponent faster.

• Quicker close quarter combat techniques means better grappling, clinching and ground fighting skills.

One of the most effective methods of enhancing the physical speed of your offensive and defensive techniques is to avoid tensing your body and simply relax your muscles prior to executing your movement. Another way of developing blistering speed is to practice a particular technique thousands of times until the psychomotor movement is sharpened and crystallized. Also, proper breathing will optimize psychomotor speed.

Impact Power
In street combat, the War Machine hits his adversary with the power equivalent of a 12 gauge shotgun. Impact power refers to the amount of force you can generate when striking your opponent's targets. Contrary to popular belief, punching and kicking power is not simply predicated on size, strength or body

weight. There are other significant factors like power generator mastery, follow-through and tool velocity that also play a critical role.

For example, one crucial factor of punching power is learning to develop proper punching technique or "body mechanics" and it can be accomplished through proper training. Remember, when it come to real world combat you must be capable of striking your opponent with knock out force. To put in bluntly, You have got to hit him hard!

Punching Power
Punching power separate the men from the boys and when it comes to the true art of delivering a power punch there's a lot of misinformation out there. For example, the power punching techniques of karate are static, mechanical and lack the fluidity for overall efficiency. While at the same time, the punching power mechanic used in boxing and mixed martial arts often lack the bone shattering force necessary to knock out a powerful opponent. Believe it or not, some martial arts claim that power punching can be achieved from your inner chi!

The heavy bag or "punching bag" is the best piece of equipment for developing your punching power. Many boxing and martial arts equipment manufacturers make excellent heavy bags that can withstand the most punishing of blows. Remember, if you are looking to increase punching power for self defense purposes do not train on anything less than 75 pounds. When it comes to punching bags, the heavier the better!

Here are some points to keep in mind when developing punching power on the heavy bag.

First and foremost, know the proper way to make a fist. It's ironic how some of the most experienced street fighters and martial artists don't know how to make a proper fist. Improper fist clenching can be disastrous for some of the following reasons: (1) you can jam, sprain, or break your fingers; (2) you will destroy wrist alignment, resulting in a sprained or broken wrist; or (3) you'll lose significant power when striking. To make a proper fist, tightly clinch the four fingers evenly in the palm of your hand. Make certain that your thumb is wrapped securely around your second and third knuckles and flexed down toward the wrist.

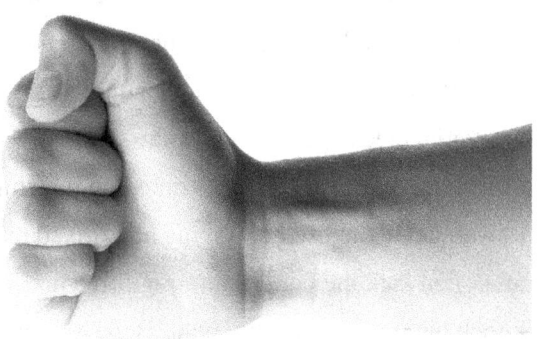

Pictured here, the proper way to make a fist.

Stay balanced when power punching on the heavy bag. Always maintain proper punching form and do not overextend your body when delivering punches and strikes. Losing your balance when delivering a power punch can be disastrous in a self defense situation. Always keep your feet directly under yourself and control your body when your transfer weight.

Be mobile and avoid the tendency to remain stationary when working out on the heavy bag. This doesn't mean that you have to dance around the punching bag like Muhammad Ali or Sugar Ray Leonard, just move around strategically and vary the speed and direction of your footwork.

Stay relaxed and try to avoid tensing your muscles when punching the bag. Tensing your muscles will significantly slow you down, lead to a possible injury and telegraph you power punch to your opponent.

Don't Lock your elbows when throwing linear punches, be certain not to lock your elbows. Elbow locking is a common problem among martial art novices. When delivering a linear blow, your arm should be extended toward its target until the elbow is not more than three inches short of full extension. After contact is made with the target, the fist is returned back to the hand guard position. Remember, if your elbow locks upon impact, it will have a pushing effect and rob you of critical punching power.

Remember to use all three power generators when delivering hand techniques from a stationary position. Essentially, power generators that will allow you to torque your body maximally. They include the following: (1) shoulders, (2) hips, and (3) feet. Maximally torquing your body into the blow will increase both the force and penetration of the blow. However, there is a very fine line between power and speed in relation to the three anatomical power generators.

When executing linear blows (lead straights, rear crosses, finger jabs, palm heels), remember that your line of initiation should always be your line of retraction. Avoid arcing or dropping your blow. Such sloppy body mechanics will throw you off balance, minimize your impact power, and open you up for a possible counterattack. Failing to maintain a straight-line trajectory is usually caused from the following: (1) your elbow does not travel behind your punch, (2) premature wrist torque.

Avoid telegraphing your strikes. Telegraphing means inadvertently making your intentions known to your assailant. There are many subtle forms of telegraphing that must be avoided in a street fight. Here are just a few:

- Cocking your arm back prior to punching or striking.
- Tensing your neck, shoulders, or arms prior to striking.
- Widening your eyes or raising your eyebrows.
- Shifting your shoulders.
- Grinning or opening your mouth.
- Taking a sudden and deep breath.

Always keep your wrists straight when throwing punching tools (circular or linear), make certain your wrists are correctly aligned with your forearm. If your wrist bends or collapses on impact, you will either sprain or break it. Remember, a sprained or broken wrist will put you out of commission immediately when fighting. When used properly, the heavy bag will train you to keep your wrists straight when delivering powerful punches in the heat of battle.

Throw different "logical" combinations on the punching bag and avoid delivering one power punch at a time. Learn to harmoniously integrate your kicks, punches and strikes into devastating and logical compound attacks that you would apply in a realistic self defense situation. This means that you must know and understand the various ways of exploiting your assailants physiological reactions dynamics.

Take your time when performing power punches on the heavy bag. Full-force power punches are unforgiving on your hands, wrist, and arms. One mistake by skeletal misalignment could instantly spell disaster for you. Always remember to progressively build up your intensity and power over a period of time. Hitting the heavy bag too hard and too soon can quickly lead to a serious hand or arm injury.

Ambidexterity

The War Machine is able to fight his adversary with equal ability on both the right and left sides of his body. Here are three important reasons why ambidexterity is essential for combat. First, your strong hand or leg might be injured or wounded in combat. Second, you might be assaulted on the weak side of your body. Third, your strong (or dominant) hand or leg might be occupied at the time of the assault.

Ambidexterity must also be mastered in the following components of combat:

- Stances - both armed and unarmed combat stances.
- Submission Holds - in both vertical and horizontal grappling planes.

- Offensive Body Weapons - kicks, punches, and various other striking techniques.
- Defensive Body Weapons - blocks, parries, and various other body evasion skills.
- Knives and Edged Weapon Skills.
- Makeshift Weapon Skills.
- Stick and Bludgeon Skills.
- Firearm Skills.

Offensive Reaction Time

The War Machine possesses an accurate sense of timing. Timing refers to your ability to execute a technique or movement at the precise moment. There are two types of timing that are used in street combat: defensive reaction time and offensive reaction time.

Defensive Reaction Time (DRT) is defined as the elapsed time between the opponent's physical attack and your defensive response to that attack.

Offensive Reaction Time (ORT) refers to the elapsed time between offensive recognition and offensive execution. Your offensive reaction time is the result of three stages (Offensive Recognition, Offensive Selection, and Offensive Execution).

1. Offensive Recognition is the first stage where you recognize and identify the ability to attack the opponent.

2. Offensive Selection is the second stage where you immediately select the appropriate offensive tool or technique.

3. Offensive Execution is the third stage where your body executes the appropriate offensive tool or technique.

Some of the best ways of developing offensive timing are through intense sparring and ground pounding sessions, double-end bag training and various focus mitt drills. Mental visualization is also another effective method of enhancing your combative timing.

Balance

Balance is the ability to maintain equilibrium while attacking and defending. You can maintain your balance in combat by controlling your center of gravity, mastering body mechanics and maintaining proper skeletal alignment.

To develop a better sense of balance, perform your body weapons slowly in front of a mirror so you become acquainted with the different weight distributions, body positions, and mechanics of each particular technique. Also, remember that balance is often lost due to weak body mechanics, poor kinesthetic perception, unnecessary weight shifting, excessive follow-through and improper skeletal alignment.

Non-Telegraphic Movement

It is critical not to telegraph or forewarn your opponent of your intentions to strike. Telegraphing means inadvertently making your offensive intentions known to your adversary. In street combat, you must posses "clean" body mechanics that don't inform your adversary of your combative agenda. Basically, all of your movements have be non-telegraphic.

There are many forms of telegraphing which need to be purged from your arsenal. Here are a few examples: staring at your selected target, chambering your arm back before striking, clenching your fists prior to punching, tensing any part of your torso, grinning or opening your mouth, widening your eyes or raising your eyebrows and taking a sudden, deep breath.

Relaxation

The War Machine's body is relaxed (but ready) during a threatening situation. Your body must also be free from muscular tension and the psychological pressure of combat. There are five effective ways to reduce nervous tension and enhance physical relaxation during a fight.

- Preparation - be prepared to handle the myriad of combat situations.
- Proper breathing - control and pace your breathing during the threatening encounter.
- Fight-or-flight response - control your fight-or-flight response by unleashing your killer instinct at the proper time.
- Proper attitude - always maintain a positive attitude during a threatening situation.
- Kinesthetic perception - kinesthetic perception is important because it allows you to effectively regulate or monitor the muscular tension in your body.

The First Strike Principle

Whenever you are faced with a threatening adversary and there is no way to escape the situation, you should strike first, strike fast, strike with authority and keep the pressure on. This combative strategy is known as the **First Strike Principle** (FSP), and it's essential to neutralize a redoubtable adversary in combat.

Essentially, a first strike is defined as the strategic application of proactive force designed to interrupt the initial stages of an assault before it becomes a self-defense situation. This offensive strategy is crucial because it allows you to innervate your enemy swiftly while at the same time precluding his capability to effectively retaliate. No time is wasted and no unnecessary risks are taken.

One inescapable fact about street combat is the longer the fight lasts, the greater your chances of serious injury or even death. Common sense suggests that you must end the street fight as quickly as possible. Striking first is the best method of achieving this combat objective because it permits you to neutralize your adversary swiftly while at the same time precluding his ability to effectively retaliate. No time is wasted and no unnecessary risks are taken.

The element of surprise is invaluable. Launching the first strike gives you the upper hand because it allows you to attack the adversary suddenly and unexpectedly. As a result, you demolish his defenses and ultimately take him out of the fight.

Switching to Auto Pilot

The War Machine has a natural instinct for combat. In the thick of battle, he delivers a whirlwind of violence that requires his energy but not his conscious thought. Since he's mastered the tools of combat, he doesn't have to think about the specific body mechanics of fighting. He doesn't have to "try hard" to execute the proper technique at the ideal moment. His body goes into a state of **auto pilot**.

You must be capable of delivering an offensive assault on your enemy without the interference of conscious thought. Combat is the last place that you want to give yourself technical instructions (i.e., thinking about striking the opponent, how to parry a jab, how to disarm a firearm). While tactics require thought, the actual application of tactics do not!

The only true way to possess the autopilot skill is through weapon and technique mastery. You must take the time to master all the offensive and defensive skills of both armed and unarmed combat. Ultimately, you must be able to unconsciously apply these skills without thought or analysis. They must be an extension of your mind, body and soul. Simply put, they must be instinctual! When it comes to tool deployment in combat, analysis often leads to paralysis!

The Killer Instinct

Self defense tools and techniques alone won't prepare you for the violence and other horrors of street fighting. A self defense technician must have a combative mentality to channel a destructiveness exceeding that of a deadly and evil criminal aggressor. He must be a cold and vicious animal free of fear, anger, apprehension, and ego. This mentality results from mastery of the killer instinct. Contemporary Fighting Arts (CFA) strives to develop the killer instinct in the self defense technician.

Unfortunately, some martial arts overlook this combative mentality. Many find it to be an unsavory concept unworthy of their civilized dojo or studios. In some martial art schools, the combative mentality violates their religious and philosophical beliefs. Other systems make the mistake of replacing the combative mentality with a "competitive" mentality. This sport-oriented mind set simply lacks the brutal and aggressive characteristics necessary to neutralize a crazed criminal attacker.

Everyone has a killer instinct!

Everyone has a killer instinct. That's just the way it is; it's how we're made. In some it may be stronger than in others. Some manifest this instinct in gross abominations. Some never call upon it at all, but it's there. Most people manifest the killer instinct in blind rage and haphazard fury. Self-defense practitioners driven by a raw killer instinct are inferior and undisciplined warriors. Their energies are poisoned by emotion, resulting in poor body mechanics and tactical errors.

On the other hand, the self-defense practitioner who has tapped into the deep reservoir of emotional calm and mental clarity of the killer instinct can open the gates of deadly destructiveness at will. Guided by virtue and courage, one can release a most destructive energy, free of emotions. This may sound paradoxical and extreme to some. But there is, in fact, no inherent incompatibility. The advanced combat warrior must be virtuous and yet altogether capable of unleashing a controlled explosion of viciousness and brutality.

The killer instinct is predicated on being emotionless. A warrior must not experience emotions while engaged with his adversary. He must temporarily eliminate fear, anger, remorse, and ego from his conscious. Molding the average person into an emotionless warrior is not an easy task. We are, in fact, emotional creatures who, from childhood, are conditioned to feel for ourselves and others. Humans are expressive beings, crying when hurt, laughing when happy, yelling when angry. Emotional expressions are integral to our growth and development. They are, in part, the essence of humanity. It's against our nature to be otherwise. However, it's essential that the warrior remain emotionless during a violent confrontation because emotions create indecisiveness and dangerous tactical vulnerabilities.

The modern warrior must not fear death or physical disfigurement. Interestingly enough, some see fear as a positive self-defense attribute, believing the so-called **"fight or flight" syndrome** will help defeat the enemy. They site superhuman feats performed out of fear or panic. Perhaps the most popular one is the story of a mother who lifts a car to free her trapped child. This may or may not be possible. Frankly, I doubt it, but in any event there is no reliable correlation between rare paranormal phenomena and the deep psychological realms of unarmed combat.

Control of the emotions also prevents anger from poisoning the warrior. Anger is a useless emotion that only taxes energy and creates numerous vulnerabilities. The famous satirist Pietro Aretino put it best when he said, *"Angry men are blind and foolish, for reason at such time takes flight and, in her absence, wrath plunders all the riches of the intellect, while the judgment remains the prisoner of its own pride."*

Viciousness is another critical characteristic of the killer instinct. By viciousness I mean dangerously aggressive behavior or extreme violence. Many people will consider this the most revolting aspect of the controlled killer instinct. However, if a martial artist is to prevail in combat, he must be more vicious than his adversary. His tools and techniques must be brutal, explosive, and conclusive. At the same time, his attack must be strategically calculated to maximize efficiency, effectiveness and safety.

The killer instinct also requires a unified mind. A unified mind is one that is free from distractions and fully focused on the enemy. Distractions are derived from two sources. The first is internal, wherein your mind wanders off or panics prior to or during actual combat. The second is external, when your adversary attempts to verbally "psych you out," for example. Environmental conditions such as weather, lighting, terrain, and noise can also create external distractions. Regardless of the source, distractions must be ignored and eliminated from your consciousness.

There are various other characteristics of the killer instinct that must not be overlooked. They include: lucid thinking, heightened situational awareness, adrenaline surge, physical mobilization, psychomotor control, absence of distractions, unified mind, courage, tactical implementation, breath control, pseudospeciation and pain tolerance.

The bottom line is when harnessed, disciplined, and forged, the killer instinct is a tremendous source of power. Developing and refining this essential combative mentality is not an easy task. It requires the application of specific cognitive exercise in conjunction with intense combat training provided by a competent "reality based" self defense instructor.

Natural Body Weapons

A War Machine must posses the knowledge, skills, and attitude necessary to utilize the complete hierarchy of weapons. The hierarchy of weapons for both armed and unarmed combat are as follows:

- Natural body weapons
- Sticks and bludgeons
- Chemical irritants
- Make-shift weapons
- Knives and edged weapons
- Firearms

For purposes of this book I am going to only address natural body weapons.

The 14 Natural Body Weapons

Natural body weapons are the various body parts that can be used to disable, cripple, or kill your criminal enemy. For reasons of simplicity, I have identified fourteen that can be used in a real world self defense situation. Once again, they are based on efficiency, effectiveness and overall safety for the practitioner. There are fourteen that you must be aware of and they are as follows:

Head- When fighting in grappling range, your head can be used for butting your opponent's nose. Keep in mind that the head butt can be delivered in four different directions: forward, backward, right side, and left side.

Teeth - The teeth can be used for biting anything on your opponent's body (nose, ears, throat, fingers, etc.) Remember to bite deeply into the assailant's flesh and shake your head vigorously. While a deep penetrating bite is extremely painful, it also transmits a powerful psychological message to your assailant. It lets him know that you mean business and are willing to do anything to survive.

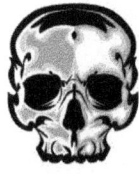
Warning: *There is an important concern to biting in a street fight: you run the risk of contracting AIDS if your adversary is infected and you draw blood while biting him.*

When executed properly, the head butt can be a devastating strike. Here, Sammy Franco delivers a ramming head butt to his assailant's chin.

Voice - Believe it or not but your voice is a very powerful tool. When fighting, the yell is a natural manifestation of the voice. Yelling actually serves several strategic purposes in combat. Yelling while fighting can distract, startle, and temporarily paralyze your assailant. It can cause the adversary to freeze in his tracks, allowing you a split second advantage to deliver the first debilitating strike and thus gain offensive control. Yelling can also be used to psych-out the assailant. It also synchronizes your state of mind with the physical process taking place. It is the catalyst that sets off the killer instinct. It is the primal expression that harbors the killer instinct. In addition, yelling actually may draw attention to your fight.

Elbows - The elbows are devastating weapons that can generate tremendous power. Elbow strikes can be delivered vertically, diagonally and horizontally to the opponent's nose, temple, chin, throat, solar plexus and ribs.

Fists - The fists are used for punching the opponent's temple, nose, chin, throat, solar plexus, ribs and in some cases, the groin. However, punching is a true art form that requires considerable training and practice to master.

Palms - The heel of your palm can be used for delivering palm heel strikes. A strike of the palm can be exceptionally powerful and it is best delivered on a 45-degree angle to the opponent's nose or chin.

There's good reason why the fist is considered by many to be universal sign of aggression. It's a staple natural body weapon.

Fingers/Nails - Your fingers and nails can be used for jabbing, clawing and gouging the opponent's eyes. They can also be used for pulling, tearing and crushing the opponent's throat and testicles.

Edge of Hand - The edge of your hand can be whipped horizontally into the opponent's nose or throat, causing severe injury or death. It can also be delivered vertically to the assailant's nose or diagonally to the back of your opponent's neck.

Web of Hand - The web of your hand can be used to deliver web hand strikes to the opponent's throat. When striking, be certain to keep your hand stiff with your palm facing down.

Knees - The knees are excellent grappling range weapons that can bring down the most powerful of adversaries.

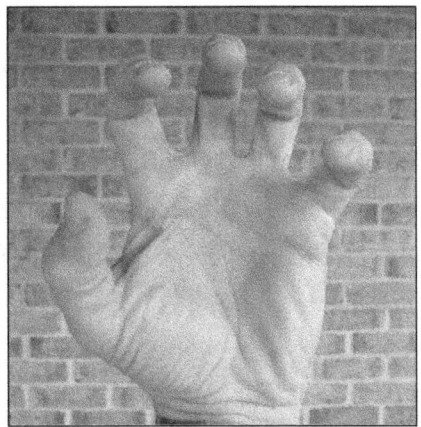

Believe it or not, the fingers can be a devastating natural body weapon that can tear, crush, rip and gouge soft tissue targets.

Knee strikes can be delivered vertically and diagonally to the opponent's thigh, groin, ribs, solar plexus and face.

Shins - The shinbone is another powerful body weapon that can quickly cripple your assailant. When striking with your shin, aim for the opponent's thigh, the side of his knee, or groin.

Insteps - The instep is used for delivering vertical kicks to the opponent's groin and-in some cases-his head. The instep is a good impact tool because it increases the power of your kick, prevents broken toes, and also lengthens the surface area of your natural body weapon.

Heel of Foot - The heel of your foot is used for delivering side kicks to the opponent's thigh, knee or shin. It can also be used to stomp down on the assailant's toes.

Ball of Foot - The ball of your foot is used for delivering push kicks into your opponent's thigh. It can also be used to deliver a quick snap kick into the assailant's shin bone.

The instep is extremely strong and can deliver a devastating kick. In this photo, a vertical kick is delivered to the knife attacker's chin. This technique is called "punting" and it is only permitted in self defense situations that warrant the use of deadly force.

PART IV
War Machine Philosophy

"The end and aim of the Cynic philosophy, as indeed of every philosophy, is happiness, but happiness that consists in living according to nature, and not according to the opinions of the multitude." -Flavius Claudius Julianus

"REVENGE CAN BE AN HONORABLE TRAIT."

"WHEN YOUR MIND, BODY AND SPIRIT FUSE INTO AN EFFICIENT AND UNEMOTIONAL WEAPON, YOU WILL BECOME THE WARRIOR."

"IT IS BETTER TO DIE WITH DIGNITY THAN TO LIVE WITH DISHONOR."

"APPROACH COMBAT IN TERMS OF BLACK AND WHITE, BUT BE PREPARED FOR GRAY."

"NEVER UNDERESTIMATE THE VICIOUS CAPABILITY OF A HUMAN BEING."

"AGGRESSIVE ACTION WINS."

"EVERY BATTLE MUST BE WON FAST."

"COMBAT BEGINS WHERE DIPLOMACY ENDS."

"STRICT ADHERENCE TO TRADITIONAL PERSPECTIVES WILL ALMOST GUARANTEE YOU DEATH IN A REAL FIGHT."

"REACHING THE PINNACLE OF COMBATIVE COMPETENCY DOES NOT OCCUR THROUGH SOME MYSTICAL TRANSFORMATION. IT'S ACQUIRED THROUGH PERSISTENCE AND LOTS OF HARD WORK."

"BEWARE OF THE EGO. HE IS A DARK BEAST DESIROUS OF DESTRUCTION."

"NEVER SHOW AN ACT OF DEFIANCE THAT YOU ARE NOT PREPARED TO DEFEND."

"A GREAT FIGHTER WILL ALWAYS ACT SWIFTLY AND DECISIVELY; HE DOESN'T KNOW THE MEANING OF APPREHENSION."

"A TRUE WARRIOR IS ALWAYS ALONE."

"SUPPORT CAPITAL PUNISHMENT."

"NEVER TEACH THE ART OF COMBAT TO ANYONE ON THE WRONG SIDE OF THE LAW."

"FRUSTRATION AND TIME ARE THE GATEKEEPERS THAT SEPARATE THE TYRO FROM THE EXPERT."

"DESPAIR IS ALWAYS ONE STEP AWAY FROM DEATH."

"THERE ARE NO ABSOLUTES IN COMBAT."

"A STUPID MAN DIES A STUPID DEATH."

"TRAIN FOR THE EXCEPTION AS WELL AS THE RULE."

"ORDER AND JUSTICE CAN ONLY BE EXECUTED THROUGH A HAND OF MIGHT."

"QUESTION AUTHORITY; JUST DO IT RESPECTFULLY."
"NEVER BETRAY A FRIEND."

"THERE IS NO HONOR IN DEFEAT."

"COMBATIVE TRUTH IS NOT RELATIVE. IT'S A FACT."

"FOR EVERY ATTACK, THERE IS A LOGICAL COUNTER."
"DON'T RESPECT PACIFISTS OR FIGHT FOR THEM."

"WHAT YOU DO NOT KNOW CAN CERTAINLY GET YOU KILLED."

"KNOWLEDGE IS USELESS UNLESS IT IS PUT INTO ACTION."

"A WAR IS NEVER REALLY OVER."

"JUSTICE IS NOT ALWAYS SERVED."

"THE MORE YOU KNOW, THE LESS YOU WILL FEAR."

"SUCCESS AND FAILURE TRANSLATE TO LIFE AND DEATH IN BATTLE."

"A FORMIDABLE WARRIOR IS A COLD AND VICIOUS ANIMAL, ALBEIT AN INTELLIGENT ONE."

"BEWARE OF THE CALL OF VIOLENCE AND BE EVER VIGILANT OF THE EGO'S CHARMS."

"COMBAT FORMLESSNESS IS THE FETUS OF DEATH."

"A WARRIOR MUST POLICE HIS SKILLS WITH A MORAL FABRIC CALLED HONOR."

"FEAR IS ESTABLISHED WHEN IGNORANCE IS ACTUALIZED."
"DEFEND THE WEAK."

"EXPERIMENTATION IN THE FACE OF DANGER IS AN INVITATION TO DISASTER."

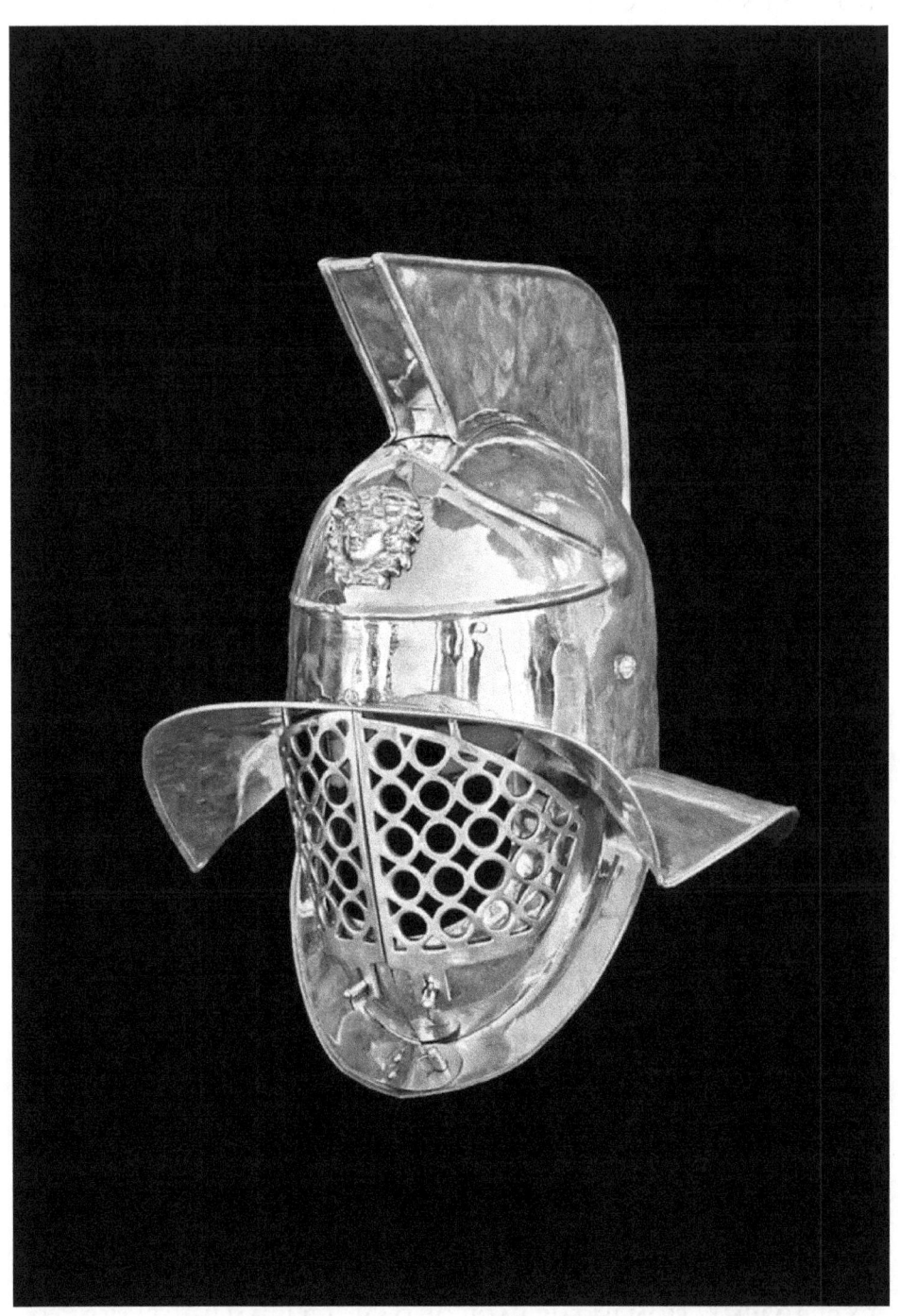

"IT TAKES A LIFETIME TO MASTER A CREDIBLE SYSTEM OF COMBAT."

"VIOLENCE IS A DARK CLOAK THAT YOU MUST WEAR EVEN IF YOU DON'T LIKE THE WAY IT FITS."

"AS LONG AS HUMANKIND WALKS THE EARTH, THERE WILL ALWAYS BE A TIME, NEED, AND PLACE FOR COMBAT."

"LIFE BETRAYS EVERYONE."

"THE FIRST CASUALTY OF BATTLE IS THE EGO."

"NEVER, EVER FORGIVE EVIL."

"THOSE WHO SPEAK THE TRUTH ARE NEVER LIKED."

"FEAR KILLS A WARRIOR TWICE."

"THE ONLY THING THAT STANDS BETWEEN YOU AND DEATH IS YOUR ABILITY TO FIGHT."

"LIVE EVERY DAY AS IF IT WERE YOUR LAST."

"A PACIFIST IS A MAN WHO IS TOO COWARDLY TO FIGHT AND TOO FAT TO RUN."

"ALL GREAT WARRIORS ARE SLAVES OF PERFECTION."

"MAKE SURE YOU KNOW THE LAWS AND RULES OF COMBAT BEFORE YOU ATTEMPT TO CRITICIZE THEM."

"SELF-DEFENSE IS NOT JUST A RIGHT; IT'S YOUR RESPONSIBILITY."

"IN COMBAT, IT IS ALWAYS BETTER TO ACT THAN REACT."

"TRUTH GIVES YOU THE POWER TO MAKE THINGS BETTER."
"TRUST IN GOD."

"NOTHING IS SACRED IN COMBAT."

"THE LONGER A FIGHT LASTS, THE GREATER YOUR CHANCES OF INJURY OR DEATH."

"ATTACK EVEN WHEN YOU RETREAT."

"THOSE WHO REJECT THE NECESSITY OF VIOLENCE REJECT THE NECESSITY OF PEACE."

"FOOLS RUSH INTO COMBAT."

"ALTHOUGH COMBAT PREPAREDNESS IS CRITICAL TO YOUR SURVIVAL, NEVER FORGET THE IMPORTANCE OF LOVE, LIFE, AND LAUGHTER."

"WHEN DANGER IS IMMINENT, STRIKE FIRST, STRIKE FAST, STRIKE HARD AND KEEP THE PRESSURE ON."

"TO TRULY MASTER THE ESSENCE OF COMBAT, YOU MUST STUDY IT AS A SCIENCE AND EXPRESS IT AS AN ART."

Appendix A: Battle Casualties

Although the War Machine is a ferocious combatant, there's always the possibility that he can become injured. Here are several important emergency/first aid guidelines.

Once the fight is over and you have fled the scene safely, conduct a quick inventory of your body. Quickly scan your torso, hands, arms, legs, and feet for any possible signs of injury. Run both hands down your face and over your head and neck to check for blood. This is important because many times fighters are seriously injured after a fight and don't even know it because the adrenaline rush from the fight-or-flight response shuts off the pain.

If you find that you are injured after a fight, seek medical assistance immediately. Have a good friend drive you to the hospital or dial 911 and request an ambulance. Stay calm, breathe slowly, and tell the emergency dispatcher your exact location. If you are bleeding heavily, apply direct pressure to the wound site. If the wound is located in a limb, elevate the extremity above the level of the heart. This will slow down the loss of blood. If you get cut or shot in the leg, do not try to stand up or walk. This will worsen the injury and increase the loss of blood.

If you have sustained a gunshot wound, first cover the wound with a clean cloth or your bare hands. If there are entry wounds and exit wounds, try to cover both of them. Once the bleeding has slowed down, bandage the wound and get medical assistance immediately.

If you have the terrible misfortune of having a knife wound, first stabilize the weapon. Do not pull it out! Leave the knife where it is and seek medical treatment immediately. Many street fighters have walked into hospital emergency rooms with a knife stuck in a major organ and survived because of tamponading. Tamponading occurs when the surrounding organ tissue surrounds the blade, and therefore the blood loss slows down dramatically.

If you have broken a bone or torn a joint, immobilize the limb immediately. This will reduce the pain and prevent further injury to the afflicted area. These are just a few suggestions that will buy you some time before the ambulance arrives.

Appendix B: Code of Conduct

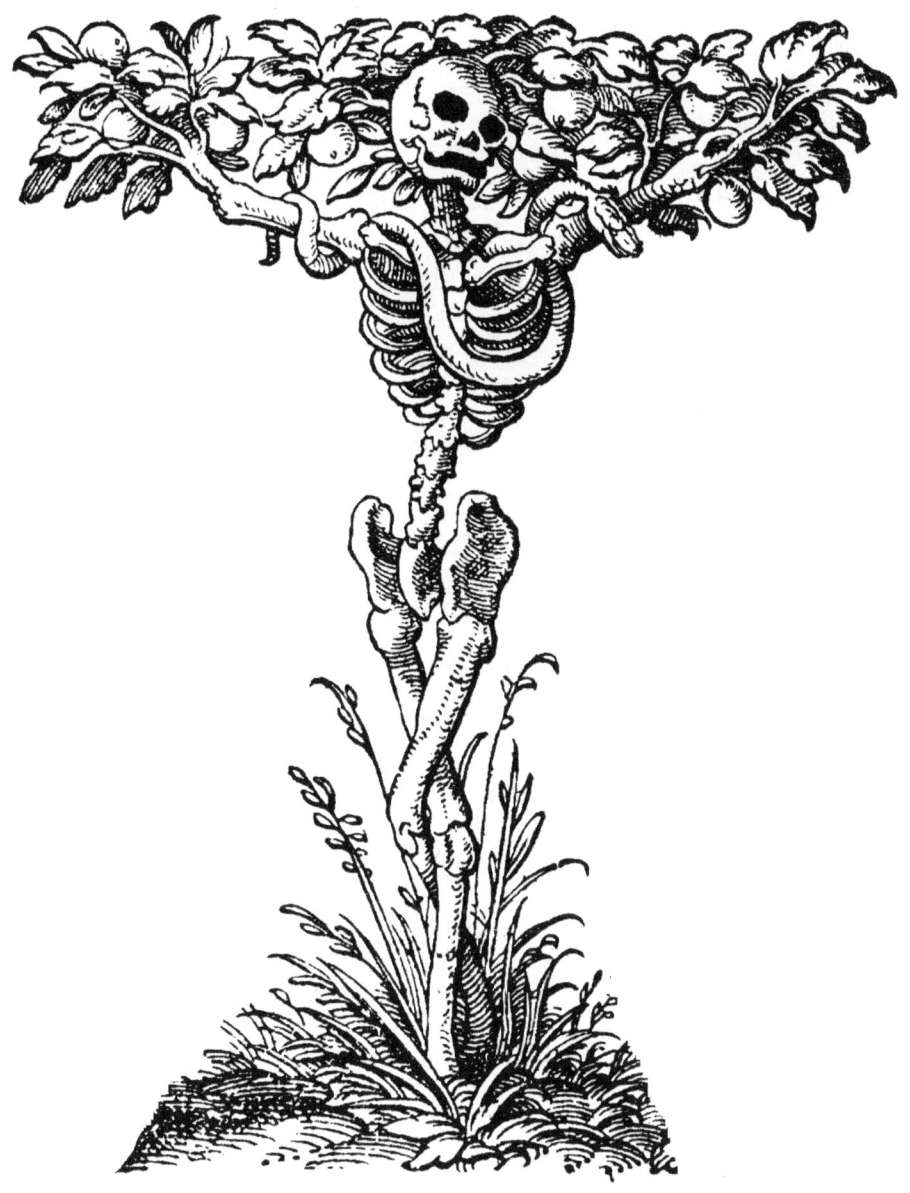

- Be loyal to family, friends and country.

- Be fearless in the face of danger.

- Carry yourself with dignity and grace.

- Be tenacious with all of your endeavors.

- Be decisive and stick to your convictions and beliefs.

- Don't genuflect or prostrate to another.

- Have compassion for the weak or handicapped.

- Be self-confident at all times.

- Be accountable for all of your actions.

- Obey the law.

- Don't abuse your body with controlled substances.

- Admit when you are wrong.

- Be skeptical yet open-minded.

- Reject complacency.

- Never feel sorry for yourself.

- Never make the same mistake twice.

- Always speaks the truth.

- Don't be concerned what others may think of you.

- Never succumbs to the trappings of immediate gratification.

Cold indifference drenches my face
As blue heavens turn to dust
I am banished by the human race
For my dark soul craves violent lust
Oh grant me this rightful dream of hate
In which flesh and bone sear with pain
The clock ticks on until its too late
And those who oppose me lie fallen slain

- WAR MACHINE CHRONICLES
Chapter XX, Verse 3

War Machine Glossary

The following terms are defined within the context of Contemporary Fighting Arts and its related concepts. In some instances, the definitions bear little resemblance to those found in a standard English dictionary.

Ability – One of the three components that constitute jeopardy. Ability means the enemy has the ability to cause you or another person grievous bodily harm or death. (See opportunity and intent.)

Accuracy - The precise or exact projection of force. Accuracy is also defined as the ability to execute a combative movement with precision and exactness.

Adaptability - The ability to physically and psychologically adjust to new or different conditions or circumstances of combat.

Adrenaline Dump - The process of adrenaline (also called epinephrine) being rapidly released into your blood stream in response to a fighting situation.

Advanced First Strike Tools - Offensive techniques specifically used to initiate a first strike against multiple opponents.

Aerobic Exercise - "With air." Exercise that elevates the heart rate to a training level for a prolonged period of time, usually 30 minutes.

Aesthetic Intimidation- The ability to intimidate your enemy through your physical appearance.

Aggression - Hostile and injurious behavior directed toward a person.

Aggressive Hand Positioning - Placement of hands so as to imply aggressive or hostile intentions.

Agility - An attribute of combat. One's ability to move his or her body quickly and gracefully.

Ambidextrous - The ability to perform with equal facility on both the right and left sides of the body.

Anabolic Steroids – Synthetic chemical compounds that resemble the male sex hormone called testosterone. This "performance-enhancing" drug is known to increase muscle mass, strength and endurance in most athletes.

Analysis and Integration - One of the five elements of CFA's mental component. This is the painstaking process of breaking down various elements, concepts, sciences, and disciplines into their atomic parts, and then methodically and strategically analyzing, experimenting, and drastically modifying the information so that it fulfills three combative requirements: efficiency, effectiveness and safety. Only then is it finally integrated into the CFA system.

Anatomical Striking Targets - The various anatomical body targets that can be struck and which are especially vulnerable to potential harm. They include: the eyes, temple, nose, chin, back of neck, front of neck, solar plexus, ribs, groin, thighs, knees, shins, and instep.

Assailant - A person who threatens or attacks another person.

Assault - The willful attempt or threat to inflict injury upon the person of another.

Assault and Battery - The unlawful touching of another person without justification.

Assessment - The process of rapidly gathering, analyzing, and accurately evaluating information in terms of threat and danger. You can assess people, places, actions, and objects.

Attack - Offensive action designed to physically control, injure, or kill another person.

Attack Recognition - The first stage of defensive reaction time where you realize and identify that an attack has occurred.

Attributes of Combat - The physical, mental, and spiritual qualities that enhance combat skills and tactics.

Auto Pilot – The skill and ability to fight effectively without conscious thought.
Awareness - Perception or knowledge of people, places, actions, and objects. (In CFA there are three categories of tactical awareness: Criminal Awareness, Situational Awareness, and Self-Awareness.)

Balance - One's ability to maintain equilibrium while stationary or moving.

Blading the Body - Strategically positioning your body at a 45-degree angle from the enemy.

Block - A defensive tool designed to intercept the assailant's attack by placing a non-vital target between the assailant's strike and your vital body target.

Bludgeon Defense Stance – A strategic stance assumed when one is faced with a bludgeon-wielding enemy.

Body Composition - The ratio of fat to lean body tissue.

Body Language - Nonverbal communication through posture, gestures, and facial expressions.

Body Mechanics - Technically precise body movement during the execution of a body weapon, defensive technique, or other fighting maneuver.

Body Weapon - One of the various body parts that can be used to strike or otherwise injure or kill a criminal assailant. (Also known as tool.)

Breakdown Reaction – One of the four stress-related phenomena that an untrained fighter will experience. Breakdown Reaction occurs when a fighter's body breaks down during the combat situation. (Also see, surprise reaction, distraction reaction, and distortion reaction.)

Burnout – A negative emotional state acquired by physically over training. Some symptoms of burnout include: physical illness, boredom, anxiety, disinterest in training and general sluggishness.

Cadence - Coordinating tempo and rhythm to establish a timing pattern of movement.

Cardiorespiratory Conditioning - The component of physical fitness that deals with the heart, lungs, and circulatory system.

Centerline - An imaginary vertical line that divides your body in half and which contains many of your vital anatomical targets.

Circular Movement - Movements that follow the direction of a curve.

Close Quarter Combat – The closest distance of both armed and unarmed combat.

Cognitive Development - One of the five elements of CFA's mental component. The process of developing and enhancing your fighting skills through specific mental exercises and techniques. (see analysis and integration, killer instinct, philosophy and strategic/tactical development.)

Cognitive Exercises - Various mental exercises used to enhance fighting skills and tactics.

Combative Arts - The various arts of war. (See martial arts.)

Combative Attributes - (See attributes.)

Combative Desensitization – A component of mental toughness whereby the War Machine is habituated to the gruesome residuals of combat.

Combative Fitness - A state characterized by cardiorespiratory and muscular/skeletal conditioning, as well as proper body composition.

Combative Mentality - A combative state of mind necessary for fighting. Also known as the Killer Instinct. (See killer instinct.)

Combat Ranges - The various ranges of unarmed combat.

Combative Utility - The quality of condition of being combatively useful.

Combination(s) - (See compound attack.)

Common Peroneal Nerve - A pressure point area located approximately four to six inches above the knee on the mid line of the outside of the thigh.

Composure - A combative attribute. Composure is a quiet and focused mindset that enables you to acquire your combative agenda.

Compound Attack - One of the five conventional methods of attack. Two or more body weapons launched in strategic succession whereby the fighter overwhelms his assailant with a flurry of full speed, full force blows.

Conditioning Training - A CFA training methodology requiring the practitioner to deliver a variety of offensive and defensive combinations for a four minute period (see Proficiency Training and Street Training.)

Contemporary Fighting Arts® (CFA) – An offensive based American combat system made up of three parts: physical, mental , and spiritual.

Conventional Ground Fighting Tools - Specific ground fighting techniques designed to control, restrain and temporarily incapacitate your adversary. Some conventional ground fighting tactics include: submission holds, locks, certain choking techniques, and specific striking techniques.

Coordination - A physical attribute characterized by the ability to perform a technique or movement with efficiency, balance, and accuracy.

Counterattack - Offensive action made to counter an assailant's initial attack.

Courage - A component of mental toughness. The state of mind and spirit that enables the War Machine to face danger and vicissitudes with confidence, resolution, and bravery.

Courageousness - (See courage.)

Creatine Monohydrate – A colorless and odorless training supplement that boosts strength, endurance and builds lean muscle mass.

Creative Visualization – The purposeful formation of mental images to improve your combat skills and abilities.

Criminal Awareness - One of the three categories of CFA awareness. It involves a general understanding and knowledge of the nature and dynamics of a criminal's motivations, mentalities, methods, and capabilities to perpetrate violent crime. (See situational awareness and self-awareness.)

Criminal Justice - The study of criminal law and the procedures associated with its enforcement.

Criminology - The scientific study of crime and criminals.

Cross Stepping - The process of crossing one foot in front or behind the other when moving.

Crushing Tactics - Nuclear grappling range techniques designed to crush the assailant's anatomical targets.

Cutting Makeshift Weapon – One of the four types of makeshift weapons. Any object or implement that can be used to effectively stab or slash the enemy. (Also see distracting makeshift weapon, shielding makeshift weapon, and striking makeshift weapon.)

Dead Side – When the enemy is squared-off in a stance, his dead side is the side of his body that is closest to you.

Deadly Force - Weapons or techniques that may result in imminent, unconsciousness, permanent disfigurement, or death.

Deception - A combative attribute. A stratagem whereby you delude your assailant.

Decisiveness - A component of mental toughness. The ability to follow a tactical course of action that is unwavering and focused.

De-escalation Stance – A strategic and non-aggressive stance used when defusing a hostile individual.

Defense - The ability to strategically thwart an assailant's attack (armed or unarmed).

Defensive Execution - The third and final stage of defensive reaction time where your body executes the appropriate defensive response.

Defensive Flow - A progression of continuous defensive responses.

Defensive Mentality - A defensive mind-set.

Defensive Reaction Time (DRT)- The elapsed time between the assailant's physical attack (i.e. punch, kick, throat grab, etc.) and your defensive response to that attack (i.e., block, parry, evasion movement, etc.) Defensive reaction time is the result of three stages (Attack Recognition, Defensive Selection, and Defensive Execution.)

Defensive Selection - The second stage of defensive reaction time where you immediately select the appropriate defensive response.

Demeanor - One of the essential factors to consider when assessing a threatening individual. A person's outward behavior.

Dependency – The dangerous phenomenon of solely relying on a particular person, agency, instrument, device, tool, animal, or weapon for combat or personal protection.

Diet - A life-style of healthy eating.

Distancing - The ability to quickly understand spatial relationships and how they relate to combat.

Distortion Reaction – One of the four stress-related phenomena that an untrained fighter will experience. Distortion Reaction occurs when a fighter perceives a combat situation unrealistically. (Also see, surprise reaction, breakdown reaction and distraction reaction.)

Distracting Makeshift Weapons – One of the four types of makeshift weapons. An object that can be thrown into the enemy's face, body or legs to distract him temporarily. (See cutting makeshift weapon, striking makeshift weapon, and shielding makeshift weapon.)

Distraction Reaction – One of the four stress-related phenomena that an untrained fighter will experience. Distraction reaction occurs when the fighter's mind is inundated with internal distractions resulting in self-doubt.
(Also see surprise reaction, breakdown reaction and distortion reaction.)

Distractionary Tactics - Various verbal and physical tactics designed to distract your adversary.

Effectiveness - One of the three criteria for a CFA body weapon, technique, tactic or maneuver. It means the ability to produce a desired effect (see Efficiency and Safety).

Efficiency - One of the three criteria for a CFA body weapon, technique, tactic or maneuver. It means the ability to reach an objective quickly and economically (see Effectiveness and Safety).

Emotionless - A combative attribute. Being temporarily devoid of human feeling.

Evasion - A defensive maneuver that allows you to strategically maneuver your body away from the assailant's strike.

Evasive Sidestepping - Evasive footwork where the practitioner moves to either the right or left side.

Evasiveness - A combative attribute. The ability to avoid threat or danger.

Excessive Force - An amount of force that exceeds the need for a particular event and is unjustified in the eyes of the law.

Experimentation - The painstaking process of testing a combative hypothesis or theory.

Explosiveness - A combative attribute that is characterized by a sudden outburst of violent energy.

Fear - A strong and unpleasant emotion caused by the anticipation or awareness of threat or danger. There are three stages of fear in order of intensity: Fright, Panic, and Terror. (See fright, panic, terror.)

Femoral Nerve – A pressure point area located approximately six inches above the knee on the inside of the thigh.

Fighting Stance - One of the different types of stances used in CFA's system. A strategic posture you can assume when face-to-face with an unarmed assailant (s). The fighting stance is used after you have launched your first strike tool.

Fight-or-Flight Syndrome - A response of the sympathetic nervous system to a fearful and threatening situation, during which it prepares your body to either fight or flee from the perceived danger.

Finesse - A combative attribute. The ability to skillfully execute a movement or a series of movements with grace and refinement.

First Strike - The strategic application of proactive force designed to interrupt the initial stages of an assault before it becomes a self-defense situation.

First Strike Principle (FSP) - A CFA principle which states that when physical danger is imminent and you have no other tactical option but to fight back, you should strike first, strike fast, strike with authority and keep the pressure on.

First Strike Stance - One of the different types of stances used in CFA's system. A strategic posture used prior to initiating a first strike.

First Strike Tools - Offensive tools specifically designed to initiate a preemptive strike against your adversary.

Flexibility - The muscles' ability to move through maximum natural ranges (see muscular/skeletal conditioning.)

Follow Through – A component of mental toughness. Follow-through is the ability to continue fighting regardless of the adversities that one is faced with.

Footwork - Quick, economical steps performed on the balls of the feet while you are relaxed, alert, and balanced. Footwork is structured around four general movements: forward, backward, right, and left.

Fright - The first stage of fear; quick and sudden fear (See panic and terror.)

Ghosting - The strategic process of mentally eliminating facial features on your adversary, so that he appears face-less. Ghosting is most commonly used to prevent eye staring and for pseudospeciation enhancement.

Grappling Range - One of the three ranges of unarmed combat. Grappling range is the closest distance of unarmed combat from which you can employ a wide variety of close-quarter tools and techniques. The grappling range of unarmed combat is also divided into two different planes: vertical (standing) and horizontal (ground fighting). (See kicking range and punching range.)

Grappling Range Tools - The various body tools and techniques that are employed in the grappling range of unarmed combat, including head butts; biting, tearing, clawing, crushing, and gouging tactics; foot stomps, horizontal, vertical, and diagonal elbow strikes, vertical and diagonal knee strikes, chokes, strangles, joint locks, and holds. (See and kicking range tools.)

Ground Fighting - Fighting that takes place on the ground. (Also known as horizontal grappling plane.)

Growth Pain – One of the two types of physical pain. Growth pain is a dull burning sensation that one experiences when exercising and training. (Also see injury pain.)

Guard - A fighter's hand positioning.

Habituated – To become accustom to something by frequent repetition or prolonged exposure.

Hand Positioning - (See guard.)

Hard Core Attitude – A component of mental toughness. A tough, no non-sense state of mind.

Hard Look – An essential component of the War Machine's physique which is comprised of two parts: (1) facial characteristics—his facial expressions indicate someone who is alert, dead serious, and very confident. (2) body characteristics—his physique is noticeably solid, strong, and powerful.

Head-Hunter - Strategically selecting and pursuing the opponent's head as a primary impact target.

Heavy Bag - A large cylindrical shaped bag that is used to develop kicking, punching or striking power.

High-Line Kick - One of the two different classifications of a kick. A kick that is directed to targets above an assailant's waist level. (See low-line kick.)

Histrionics - The field of theatrics or acting.

Hook Kick - A circular kick that can be delivered in both kicking and punching ranges.

Hook Punch - A circular punch that can be delivered in both the punching and grappling ranges.

Impact Power - Destructive force generated by mass and velocity.

Impact Training - A training exercise that develops pain tolerance.

Incapacitate - To disable an assailant by rendering him unconscious or damaging his bones, joints or organs.

Initiative - Making the first offensive move in combat.

Injury Pain – One of the two types of physical pain. Injury pain is a sharp and intense sensation that usually indicates damage to a tendon, ligament or muscle. (Also see growth pain.)

Inside Position – The area between both of the enemy's arms where he has the greatest amount of control.

Intent – One of the three components that constitute jeopardy. Intent means the enemy has shown a manifested intent to cause you or another person grievous bodily harm or death. (see opportunity and ability.)

Intuition - The innate ability to know or sense something without the use of rational thought.

Invisible Deployment - (see non-telegraphic movement.)

Jeopardy – A state or situation of risk or danger comprised of three elements: ability, opportunity and intent.

Joint Lock - A grappling range technique that immobilizes the assailant's joint.

Kick - A sudden, forceful strike with the foot.

Kicking Range - One of the three ranges of unarmed combat. Kicking range is the furthest distance of unarmed combat wherein you use your legs to strike an assailant. (see grappling range and punching range.)

Kicking Range Tools - The various body weapons employed in the kicking range of unarmed combat, including side kicks, push kicks, hook kicks, and vertical kicks.

Killer Instinct - A cold, primal mentality that surges to your consciousness and turns you into a vicious and deadly warrior.

Kinesics - The study of nonlinguistic body movement communications (i.e., eye movement, shrugs, facial gestures, etc.).

Kinesiology - The study of principles and mechanics of human movement.

Kinesthetic Perception - The ability to accurately feel your body during the execution of a particular movement.

Knife-Defense Stance – A strategic stance one assumes when unarmed and faced with a knife or edged weapon attacker.

Knife-Fighting Stance – A strategic stance used when one is armed with a knife or edged weapon.

Lead Side - The side of the body that faces an assailant.

Linear Movement - Movements that follow the path of a straight line.

Live Side – When the enemy is squared off in a stance, his live side is the side of the body furthest away from you. (see dead side.)

Low Maintenance Tool - Offensive and defensive tools that require the least amount of training and practice to maintain proficiency. Low maintenance tools generally don't require preliminary stretching.

Low-Line Kick - One of the two different classifications of a kick. A kick that is directed to targets below the assailant's waist level. (See high-line kick.)

Lock - (see joint lock.)

Long Range Combat – The furthest distance of both armed and unarmed combat.

Makeshift Weapon - A common everyday object that can be converted into either an offensive or defensive weapon. There are four makeshift weapon classifications: (1) cutting makeshift weapons, (2) shielding makeshift weapons, (3) distracting makeshift weapons, (4) striking makeshift weapons.

Makeshift Weapon Targets- Anatomical targets that are vulnerable to the one of the four makeshift weapon classifications.

Maneuver - To manipulate into a strategically desired position.

Masking – A component of the War Machine's attitude. Masking is the process of concealing your true feeling from a potential adversary by manipulating and managing your body language.

Mechanics - (See body mechanics.)

Mental Attributes - The various cognitive qualities that enhance your fighting skills.

Mental Component - One of the three vital components of the CFA system. The mental component includes the cerebral aspects of fighting including the Killer Instinct, Strategic & Tactical Development, Analysis & Integration, Philosophy and Cognitive Development (See physical component and spiritual component).

Mental Speed - The rate at which you can think and employ various cognitive skills in a combat situation.

Mental Toughness – A personality trait of the War Machine comprised of 10 elements: Hard Core Attitude, Self Confidence, Decisiveness, Follow- Through, Courage, Combative Desensitization, Viciousness, Self Discipline, Philosophical Resolution, and Responsibility.

Mental Visualization – (See creative visualization.)

Mid Range Combat – The mid-distance of both armed and unarmed combat.

Mobility - A combative attribute. The ability to move your body quickly and freely while balanced. (See footwork.)

Modern Martial Art - A pragmatic combat art that has evolved to meet the demands and characteristics of the present time.

Muscular Endurance - The muscles' ability to perform the same motion or task repeatedly for a prolonged period of time.

Muscular Flexibility - The muscles' ability to move through maximum natural ranges.

Muscular Strength - The maximum force that can be exerted by a particular muscle or muscle group against resistance.

Muscular/Skeletal Conditioning - An element of physical fitness that entails muscular strength, endurance, and flexibility.

Natural Body Weapons – The 14 body parts that can be used to disable, cripple, or kill a criminal adversary.

Natural Stance – A strategic stance used when approached by a suspicious person.

Neutralize - (See incapacitate.)

Neutral Zone - The distance outside of the kicking range from which neither the practitioner nor the assailant can touch the other.

Non aggressive Physiology - Strategic body language used prior to initiating a first strike.

Non telegraphic Movement - Body mechanics or movements that do not inform an assailant of your intentions. Also known as Invisible Deployment.

Nuclear Ground Fighting Tools - Specific grappling range tools designed to inflict immediate and irreversible damage. Some nuclear tools and tactics include: (1) biting tactics; (2) tearing tactics; (3) crushing tactics; (4) continuous choking tactics; (5) gouging techniques; (6) raking tactics; (7) and all striking techniques.

Offense - The armed and unarmed means and methods of attacking a criminal assailant.

Offensive Flow - A progression of continuous offensive movements or actions designed to neutralize or terminate your adversary. (See compound attack.)

Offensive Reaction Time (ORT) - The elapsed time between offensive recognition and offensive execution.

One-Mindedness - A state of deep concentration wherein you are free from all distractions (internal and external).

Opportunity - One of the three components that constitute jeopardy. Opportunity means the enemy has the opportunity to cause you or another person grievous bodily harm or death. (See ability and intent.)

Ostrich Defense - A common defensive response that a frightened fighter makes. The practitioner will look away from that which he fears (i.e. punches, kicks and strikes). His mentality is, "If I can't see it, it can't hurt me."

Over Training – (See burnout.)

Pain Tolerance - Your ability to physically and psychologically withstand pain.

Panic - The second stage of fear; overpowering fear (See fright and terror.)

Parry - A defensive technique; a quick, forceful slap that redirects an assailant's linear attack.

Patience - A combative attribute. The ability to endure and tolerate difficulty.

Perception - Interpretation of vital information acquired from your senses when faced with a potentially threatening situation.

Philosophical Resolution - The act of analyzing and answering various questions concerning the use of violence in defense of yourself and others.

Philosophy - One of the five aspects of CFA's mental component. A deep state of introspection whereby you methodically resolve critical questions concerning the use of force in defense of yourself or others.

Physical Attributes - The numerous physical qualities that enhance your combative skills and abilities.

Physical Component - One of the three vital components of the CFA system. The physical component includes the physical aspects of fighting including Physical Fitness, Weapon/Technique Mastery, and Combative Attributes (See mental component and spiritual component).

Physical Conditioning - (See combative fitness.)

Physiognomy - The art of judging human character from facial features.

Power - A physical attribute of armed and unarmed combat. The amount of force you can generate when striking an anatomical target.

Physical Fitness - (See combative fitness.)

Positioning - The spatial relationship of the assailant to the assailed person in terms of target exposure, escape, angle of attack, and various other strategic considerations.

Post Traumatic Syndrome (PTS) - A group of symptoms that may occur in the aftermath of a violent confrontation with a criminal assailant. Common symptoms of Post Traumatic Syndrome include denial, shock, fear, anger, severe depression, sleeping and eating disorders, societal withdrawal, and paranoia.

Precision - (See accuracy.)

Preemptive Strike - (See first strike.)

Premise - An axiom, concept, rule or any other valid reason to modify or go beyond that which has been established.

Proficiency Training - A CFA training methodology requiring the practitioner to execute a specific body weapon, technique, maneuver or tactic over and over for a prescribed number of repetitions (See conditioning training and street training.)

Proxemics - The study of the nature and effect of man's personal space.

Proximity - The ability to maintain a strategically safe distance from a threatening individual.

Pseudospeciation - A combative attribute. The tendency to assign subhuman and inferior qualities to a threatening assailant.

Psychological Conditioning - The process of conditioning the mind for the horrors and rigors of real combat.

Psychomotor Speed - The rate at which you can move your body (i.e., punching, blocking, evading) in a street fighting situation.

Punch - A quick, forceful strike of the fists.

Punching Range - One of the three ranges of unarmed combat. Punching range is the mid range of unarmed combat from which the fighter uses his hands to strike his assailant. (See kicking range and grappling range.)

Punching Range Tools - The various body weapons that are employed in the punching range of unarmed combat, including finger jabs, palm heel strikes, rear cross, knife hand strikes, horizontal and shovel hooks, uppercuts, and hammer fist strikes. (See grappling range tools and kicking range tools.)

Qualities of Combat - (See attributes of combat.)

Range - The spatial relationship between a War Machine and his enemy.

Range Deficiency - The inability to effectively fight and defend in all ranges (armed and unarmed) of combat.

Range Manipulation - A combative attribute. The strategic manipulation of combat ranges.

Range Proficiency - A combative attribute. The ability to effectively fight and defend in all ranges (armed and unarmed) of combat.

Ranges of Engagement - (See combat ranges.)

Ranges of Unarmed Combat - The three distances a fighter might physically engage with an assailant while involved in unarmed combat: kicking range, punching range, and grappling range.

Reaction Dynamics - The enemy's physical response to a particular tool, technique, or weapon after initial contact is made.

Reaction Time - The elapsed time between a stimulus and the response to that particular stimulus (See offensive reaction time and defensive reaction time.)

Rear Cross - A straight punch delivered from the rear hand that crosses from right to left (if in a left stance) or left to right (if in a right stance).

Rear Side - The side of the body furthest from the assailant (See lead side.)

Reasonable Force - That degree of force which is not excessive for a particular event and which is appropriate in protecting yourself or others.

Recovery Breathing - The active process of quickly restoring your breathing to its normal state.

Refinement - The strategic and methodical process of improving or perfecting.

Relocating - A street fighting tactic that requires you to immediately move to a new location (usually by flanking your adversary) after delivering a compound attack.

Repetition - Performing a single movement, exercise, strike or action continuously for a specific period.

Research - A scientific investigation or inquiry.

Responsibility - A component of mental toughness. The duty of being answerable for your own behavior.

Rhythm - Movements characterized by the natural ebb and flow of related elements.

Safety - One of the three criteria for a CFA body weapon, technique, maneuver or tactic. It means the that the tool, technique, maneuver or tactic provides the least amount of danger and risk for the practitioner (See efficiency and effectiveness.)

Secondary Strike Tools - Offensive techniques that are employed immediately after you launch a first strike.

Self-Awareness - One of the three categories of CFA awareness. Knowing and understanding yourself. This includes aspects of yourself which may provoke criminal violence and which will promote a proper and strong reaction to an attack. (See criminal awareness and situational awareness.)

Self-Confidence - A component of mental toughness. The unshakable belief and trust in ones own skills and abilities.

Self-Discipline – A component of mental toughness. The ability to control and manage ones emotions and desires.

Self-Enlightenment - The state of knowing your capabilities, limitations, character traits, feelings, general attributes, and motivations (See self-awareness.)

Set - A term used to describe a grouping of repetitions.

Shadow Fighting - A CFA training exercise used to develop and refine your tools, techniques, and attributes of armed and unarmed combat.

Shielding makeshift Weapon - One of the four types of makeshift weapons. Any object or implement that can be used to effectively shield oneself from the enemy's attack. (Also see cutting makeshift weapon, distracting makeshift weapon, and striking makeshift weapon.)

Single Attack (AKA "simple attack") - A method of attack whereby the fighter delivers a solitary offensive strike. It may involve a series of discrete probes or one swift and powerful strike aimed at terminating the fight.

Situational Awareness - One of the three categories of CFA awareness. A state of being totally alert to your immediate surroundings, including people, places, objects, and actions. (See criminal awareness and self-awareness.)

Skeletal Alignment - The proper alignment or arrangement of your body. Skeletal Alignment maximizes the structural integrity of striking tools.

Slash – A quick, sweeping stroke of a knife. (See stab.)

Slipping - A defensive maneuver that permits you to avoid an assailant's linear blow without stepping out of range. Slipping can be accomplished by quickly snapping the head and upper torso sideways (right or left) to avoid the blow.

Snap Back - A defensive maneuver that permits you to avoid an assailant's linear and circular blow without stepping out of range. The snap back can be accomplished by quickly snapping the head backwards to avoid the assailant's blow.

Speed - A physical and mental attribute of armed and unarmed combat. The rate or measure of the rapid rate of motion or thought process. There are two types of speed: Mental and Psychomotor.

Spiritual Component - One of the three vital components of the CFA system. The spiritual component includes the metaphysical issues and aspects of existence (See physical component and mental component.)

Square-Off - To be face-to-face with a hostile or threatening assailant who is about to attack you.

Stab – A quick thrust made with a pointed weapon or implement, usually a knife.

Stance - One of the many strategic postures that you assume prior to or during armed or unarmed combat.

Stance Selection – A combative attribute. The ability to instinctually select a stance appropriate for a particular combat situation.

Standing Firearm Stance – A strategic stance you assume when standing with a handgun.

Stick Fighting Ranges – The three separate distances of stick and bludgeon combat. Long-range combat—the farthest distance at which you can only strike your assailant's hand with your stick. Midrange combat—the distance at which you can strike your assailant's head, arms, and body with your stick. Close-quarter-range combat—the third and final distance where you can strike your assailant with the butt of your weapon and you can employ a variety of elbow, knee, and head butt strikes.

Stick Fighting Stance - A strategic stance used when you're armed with a stick.

Stick Strangling – The art and skill of strangling the enemy with a stick or bludgeon.

Stopping Power – A firearm's ability to stop the enemy from continuing any further aggressive action.

Strategic Leaning – A defensive maneuver that permits you to evade a knife slash while remaining in range to counter the enemy.

Strategic Positioning – Acquiring the most advantageous position against the enemy.

Strategy - A carefully planned method of achieving your goal of engaging an assailant under advantageous conditions.

Street Fight - A spontaneous and violent confrontation between two or more individuals wherein no rules apply.

Street Fighter - An unorthodox combatant who has no formal training. His combative skills and tactics are usually developed in the street by the process of trial and error.

Street Training - A CFA training methodology requiring the practitioner to deliver explosive compound attacks for ten to twenty seconds (See conditioning training and proficiency training.)

Strength Training - The process of developing muscular strength through systematic application of progressive resistance.

Striking Art - A combat art that relies predominantly on striking techniques to neutralize or terminate a criminal attacker.

Striking Makeshift Weapon - One of the four types of makeshift weapons. Any object or implement that can be used to effectively strike the enemy. (Also see cutting makeshift weapon, distracting makeshift weapon, and shielding makeshift weapon.)

Striking Shield - A rectangular shaped shield constructed of foam and vinyl used to develop power in most of your kicks, punches and strikes.

Striking Tool - A natural body weapon that impacts with the assailant's anatomical target.

Strong Side - The strongest and most coordinated side of your body.
Structure - A definite and organized pattern.

Style - The distinct manner in which a fighter executes or performs his combat skills.

Stylistic Integration - The purposeful and scientific collection of tools and techniques from various disciplines, which are strategically integrated and dramatically altered to meet three essential criteria: efficiency, effectiveness, and combative safety.

Surprise Reaction – One of the four stress-related phenomena that an untrained fighter will experience. Surprise Reaction is when the fighter is startled and instinctively "jumps" from the noise or action of combat. (Also see, breakdown reaction, distraction reaction, and distortion reaction.)

System - The unification of principles, philosophies, rules, strategies, methodologies, tools, and techniques of a particular method of combat.

Tactic - The skill of using the available means to achieve an end.

Target Awareness - A combative attribute which encompasses 5 strategic principles: target orientation, target recognition, target selection, target impaction, and target exploitation.

Target Exploitation - A combative attribute. The strategic maximization of your assailant's reaction dynamics during a fight. Target Exploitation can be applied in both armed and unarmed encounters.

Target Impaction - The successful striking of the appropriate anatomical target.

Target Orientation - A combative attribute. Having a workable knowledge of the assailant's anatomical targets.

Target Recognition - The ability to immediately recognize appropriate anatomical targets during an emergency self-defense situation.

Target Selection - The process of mentally selecting the appropriate anatomical target for your self-defense situation. This is predicated on certain factors, including proper force response, assailant's positioning and range.

Target Stare - A form of telegraphing whereby you stare at the anatomical target you intend to strike.

Target Zones - The three areas which an assailant's anatomical targets are located. (See zone one, zone two and zone three.)

Technique - A systematic procedure by which a task is accomplished.

Telegraphic Cognizance - A combative attribute. The ability to recognize both verbal and non-verbal signs of aggression or assault.

Telegraphing - Unintentionally making your intentions known to your adversary.

Tempo - The speed or rate at which you speak.

Terminate - The act of killing.

Terror - The third stage of fear; defined as overpowering fear (see Fright and Panic).

Timing - A physical and mental attribute of armed and unarmed combat. Your ability to execute a movement at the precise moment.

Tone - The overall quality or character of your voice.

Tool - (See body weapon.)

Traditional Style/System - (See traditional martial art.)

Training Drills - The various exercises and drills aimed at perfecting combat skills, attributes, and tactics.

Unified Mind - A mind which is free and clear of distractions and focused on the combative situation.

Use of Force Response - A combative attribute. Selecting the appropriate level of force for a particular emergency self-defense situation.

Viciousness - A component of mental toughness. Dangerously aggressive behavior.

Vigilance – The act of carefully watching.

Violence - The intentional utilization of physical force to coerce, injure, cripple, or kill.

Visualization – (See creative visualization.)

War Machine - The paradigm of a warrior.

Warm-up - A series of mild exercises, stretches, and movements designed to prepare you for more intense exercise.

Weak Side - The weakest and most uncoordinated side of your body.

Weapon and Technique Mastery - A component of CFA's physical component. The kinesthetic and psychomotor development of a weapon or combative technique.

Weapon Capability - An assailant's ability to use and attack with a particular weapon.

Weight training – (See strength training.)

Yell - A loud and aggressive scream or shout used for various strategic reasons.

Zone One - Anatomical targets related to your senses, including the eyes, temple, nose, chin, and back of neck.

Zone Three - Anatomical targets related to your mobility, including thighs, knees, shins, and instep.

Zone Two - Anatomical targets related to your breathing, including front of neck, solar plexus, ribs, and groin.

About The Author

Sammy Franco is one of the world's foremost authorities on armed and unarmed combat. Highly regarded as a leading innovator in combat sciences, Mr. Franco was one of the premier pioneers in the field of "reality-based" self-  defense. Convinced of the limited usefulness of martial arts in real street fighting situations, Mr. Franco believes in the theory that the best way to change traditional thinking is to make antiquated ideas obsolete through superior methodology. His innovative ideas have made a significant contribution to changing the thinking of many in the field about how people can best defend themselves against vicious and formidable adversaries.

Sammy Franco is perhaps best known as the founder and creator of Contemporary Fighting Arts (CFA), a state-of-the-art offensive-based combat system that is specifically designed for real-world self-defense. CFA is a sophisticated and practical system of self-defense, designed specifically to provide efficient and effective methods to avoid, defuse, confront, and neutralize both armed and unarmed attackers.

After studying and training in numerous martial art systems and related disciplines and acquiring extensive firsthand experience from real "street" combat, Mr. Franco developed his first system, known as Analytical Street Fighting. This system, which was one of the first practical "street fighting" martial arts, employed an unrestrained reality-based training methodology known as Simulated Street Fighting. Analytical Street Fighting served as the foundation for the fundamental principles of Contemporary Fighting Arts and Mr. Franco's teaching methodology. CFA also draws from the concepts and principles of numerous sciences and disciplines, including police and military science, criminal justice, criminology, sociology, human psychology, philosophy, histrionics, kinesics, proxemics, kinesiology, emergency medicine, crisis management, and human anatomy.

Sammy Franco has frequently been featured in martial art magazines, newspapers, and appeared on numerous radio and television programs. Mr. Franco has also authored numerous magazine articles and editorials, and has developed a popular library of instructional DVDs and workout music.

Mr. Franco has also written numerous best-selling books, including his first book, Street Lethal, released in 1989, which was one of the first books ever written on the subject of reality based self defense. His other books include Killer Instinct, When Seconds Count, 1001 Street Fighting Secrets, First Strike, The Bigger They Are – The Harder They Fall, War Machine, War Craft, Ground War and Warrior Wisdom.

Sammy Franco's experience and credibility in the combat science is unequaled. One of his many accomplishments in this field includes the fact that he has earned the ranking of a Law Enforcement Master Instructor, and has designed, implemented, and taught officer survival training to the United States Border Patrol (USBP). He instructs members of the US Secret Service, Military Special Forces, Washington DC Police Department, Montgomery County, Maryland Deputy Sheriffs, and the US Library of Congress Police. Sammy Franco is also a member of the prestigious International Law Enforcement Educators and Trainers Association (ILEETA) as well as the American Society of Law Enforcement Trainers (ASLET) and he is listed in the "Who's Who Director of Law Enforcement Instructors."

Sammy Franco is a nationally certified Law Enforcement Instructor in the following curricula: PR-24 Side-Handle Baton, Police Arrest and Control Procedures, Police Personal Weapons Tactics, Police Power Handcuffing Methods, Police Oleoresin Capsicum Aerosol Training (OCAT), Police Weapon Retention and Disarming Methods, Police Edged Weapon Countermeasures and "Use of Force" Assessment and Response Methods. Mr. Franco is also a National Rifle Association (NRA) instructor (both police and civilian) who specializes in firearm safety, personal protection and advanced combat pistol shooting.

Mr. Franco holds a Bachelor of Arts degree in Criminal Justice from the University of Maryland. He is a regularly featured speaker at a number of professional conferences, and conducts dynamic and enlightening seminars on numerous aspects of self-defense and personal protection. Mr. Franco has instructed thousands of students in his career, including instruction on "street fighting", grappling and ground fighting, boxing and kickboxing, knife survival and knife fighting skills, multiple opponent survival skills, stick fighting skills and firearms training.

Sammy Franco teaches not only combat-proven techniques, but from the standpoint of having a firsthand understanding of the emotional, psychological and spiritual issues that arise from surviving physical violence. Having lived through street violence himself, Mr. Franco's goal is not its glorification, but to help people free themselves from violence and its costly price.

For more information about Mr. Franco and his Contemporary Fighting Arts system, you can visit his website at: www.sammyfranco.com or contact him at the following address:

Sammy Franco
P.O. Box 84028
Gaithersburg, Maryland 20883
Phone: 301-279-2244

Finis

www.ingramcontent.com/pod-product-compliance
Lightning Source LLC
Chambersburg PA
CBHW081328090426
42737CB00017B/3051